CLAPHAM, John. Smetana. J. M. Dent (dist. by Octagon, a div. of Farrar, Straus and Giroux), 1972. 161p il bibl Master musicians series) 76-39813. 8.50

Practically speaking, there are only two other major books on Smetana: Ernst Rychnovsky's *Smetana* in German (1942) and Brian Large's *Smetana* (1970). Because of the relative lack of information on Smetana, Clapham's work does fill a definite need, though one would have liked a more extensive study. While it is accurate and scholarly, this study is really quite brief. It contains a biography and discussions of Smetana's piano, chamber, and orchestral works, choral music, songs, and operas. These discussions are most helpful but the pedantic tone does not motivate one to further investigation. Good musical examples but too few of them, especially in the chapter on piano music. Includes a guide to Czech pronunciation, a chronology, a list of works, a list of persons important in Smetana's life, a postmortem, and an index. Dry reading but, nevertheless, recommended.

The Master Musicians Series

SMETANA

SERIES EDITED BY

SIR JACK WESTRUP
M.A., Hon. D.Mus.(Oxon.), F.R.C.O.
Professor Emeritus of Music, Oxford University

VOLUMES IN THE
MASTER MUSICIANS SERIES

BACH⌒Eva Mary and Sydney Grew
BEETHOVEN ⌒ Marion M. Scott
BELLINI ⌒ ⌒ Leslie Orrey
BERLIOZ ⌒ ⌒ J. H. Elliot
BRAHMS ⌒ ⌒ Peter Latham
BRUCKNER AND MAHLER ⌒
⌒ H. F. Redlich
CHOPIN ⌒ ⌒ Arthur Hedley
DEBUSSY ⌒ Edward Lockspeiser
DELIUS ⌒ ⌒ Alan Jefferson
DVOŘÁK ⌒ ⌒ Alec Robertson
ELGAR ⌒ ⌒ ⌒ Ian Parrott
HANDEL ⌒ ⌒ Percy M. Young
HAYDN ⌒ ⌒ Rosemary Hughes
LISZT ⌒ ⌒ Walter Beckett
MENDELSSOHN ⌒ Philip Radcliffe
MONTEVERDI ⌒ ⌒ Denis Arnold
MOZART ⌒ ⌒ Eric Blom
PURCELL ⌒ ⌒ Sir Jack Westrup
SCHUBERT ⌒ Arthur Hutchings
SCHUMANN ⌒ ⌒ Joan Chissell
SIBELIUS ⌒ ⌒ Robert Layton
SMETANA ⌒ ⌒ John Clapham
VAUGHAN WILLIAMS ⌒ James Day
VERDI ⌒ ⌒ Dyneley Hussey
WAGNER ⌒ ⌒ Robert L. Jacobs

In preparation:

FRANCK ⌒ ⌒ Laurence Davies
GRIEG ⌒ ⌒ ⌒ John Horton
TCHAIKOVSKY ⌒ Edward Garden

THE MASTER MUSICIANS SERIES

SMETANA

by

JOHN CLAPHAM

*With eight pages of plates
and music examples in the text*

LONDON
J. M. DENT AND SONS LTD

OCTAGON BOOKS · NEW YORK
1972

First published 1972
© Text, John Clapham, 1972

Made in Great Britain
at the
Aldine Press · Letchworth · Herts
for
J. M. DENT & SONS LTD
Aldine House · Bedford Street · London

Library of Congress Catalog Card No. 76–39813

ISBN: 0 460 03133 3

TO MY WIFE

PREFACE

While engaged on this book I have been acutely aware of the deplorable dearth of reliable information in English, German and French on this important Czech composer, and also of the lack of balance and objectivity of much that has been published on him in the Czech language. Nejedlý's monumental study, which appeared originally in four large volumes and was reprinted in seven, unfortunately stops short in Smetana's nineteenth year, and in consequence certain other books have much greater value. Hitherto Rychnovsky's biography, published in German in 1924, has been the most satisfactory single volume book on this composer, but since my book was completed Dr Brian Large's valuable and reasonably comprehensive study has appeared. My own book has come into being after my having studied many letters and other documents and having examined the whole of Smetana's music.

While engaged on this project I have been shown much kindness which I wish to acknowledge here, even if it is not possible to mention everyone by name. I am grateful to Dr Miroslav Malý and his staff at the Bedřich Smetana Museum, Prague, for their kind assistance in various ways; to the directors of the publishing division of Supraphon for permission to quote extracts from Smetana's music in editions of firms of which they are the legal successors; to the directors of the gramophone division of Supraphon and Dr Kamil Šlapák for their generous help; and to the staff of the Österreichische Nationalbibliothek for their kind co-operation. I also wish to thank Professor František Bartoš for his greatly valued assistance; Mrs Zuzana Švabinská for her kind permission to reproduce a portrait by her father; Dr Clara Thörnqvist of Göteborg and Jarmil Burghauser for the research they undertook on my behalf; Dr Lubomír Dorůžka who has helped me to acquire much source material; and Dr Ernst Levin and Dr E. H. Cameron for the interest they have shown in Smetana's medical history.

Edinburgh,   J. C.
1972.

Most consonants are pronounced approximately as in southern English, except for the following: c is similar to ts in 'hats'; g is always hard; ch is one letter, sounding as in 'loch'; j is like y in 'yes'; r is rolled. When a hook (ˇ) is placed over a consonant the sound is modified:

č   like ch in 'church'

š   represents sh

ž   like s in 'pleasure'

ř   represents the *simultaneous* sounding of a rolled r and a ž.

Consonants are softened if followed by ě, as in the name Zdeněk (pronounced Zde⁄nyek). When d, n, and t are followed by i they are softened. Softening of these letters is also indicated as follows: ď, ň, ť or ľ. When a word ends with b, d, g, h, v, z or ž, the sounds are changed to p, t, k, ch, f, s and š respectively.

Vowels are pure as in Italian and are either short (a, e, i, o, u, y) or long (á, é, í, ó, ou, ů or ú, ý). Short vowels are pronounced approxi⁄mately as follows: a like u in 'but'; e as in 'met'; i is between i in 'it' and ea in 'eat'; o as in 'for', u as in 'put'; y is similar to the Czech i. The letters l and r may serve as vowels; hence 'Vltava' has three syllables.

The first syllable of a word is stressed, even when the first vowel is short. However, a preposition draws the stress onto itself, e.g. 'v̄e Ědǐnbǔrgǔ' (in Edinburgh).

CONTENTS

CHAP.   PAGE

PREFACE vii

GUIDE TO CZECH PRONUNCIATION viii

I. MUSIC IN BOHEMIA BEFORE SMETANA 1

II. THE COMPOSER'S ANCESTRY AND YOUTH . . . 9

III. YEARS OF STRUGGLE 17

IV. SWEDISH INTERLUDE 23

V. THE FLOWERING OF CZECH NATIONALISM . . . 31

VI. HOSTILITY AND DEAFNESS 37

VII. THE FINAL PHASE 47

VIII. PIANOFORTE MUSIC 57

IX. CHAMBER MUSIC 65

X. ORCHESTRAL WORKS 71

XI. CHORAL MUSIC AND SONG 86

XII. OPERA (1): FROM 'THE BRANDENBURGERS' TO 'LIBUŠE'. 90

XIII. OPERA (2): THE LYRICAL AND ROMANTIC WORKS . 104

XIV. CHARACTERISTICS OF SMETANA'S STYLE AND HIS
ACHIEVEMENT 116

APPENDICES

A. CALENDAR 124

B. CATALOGUE OF WORKS 136

C. PERSONALIA 142

D. BIBLIOGRAPHY 147

E. SMETANA'S POST-MORTEM 150

INDEX 153

ILLUSTRATIONS

SMETANA, *c.* 1881 . . . . *Frontispiece*

facing page

KATEŘINA SMETANA IN 1858 (*oil painting by J. P. Södermark*) . . 4

SMETANA IN 1858 (*oil painting by J. P. Södermark*) 4

FIRST PAGE OF SMETANA'S LETTER TO DR L. PROCHAZKA
(*dated 11th March 1860, written in Czech*) 23

SMETANA AND HIS WIFE BETTINA IN 1860 38

SKETCH OF MAŘENKA'S 'AH! BITTERNESS! WHEN ⎫
   HEARTS HAVE TRUSTED VAINLY!' FROM 'THE ⎬ *between pages*
   BARTERED BRIDE' . . . . . . ⎪ *94 and 95*

SCENES BY J. VILÍMEK FROM 'THE BARTERED BRIDE' ⎭

FIRST PAGE OF THE SCORE OF 'FROM BOHEMIA'S   *facing page*
   FIELDS AND FORESTS' 103

SMETANA (*posthumous charcoal drawing by Max Švabinský, 1904*) . . 118

CHAPTER I

MUSIC IN BOHEMIA BEFORE SMETANA

Bohemia's geographical position in the very heart of Europe made it almost inevitable that she would be deeply involved during the passage of many centuries in some of the most momentous political upheavals of those times, as has indeed been the case. More than a thousand years ago, after the founding of the Great Moravian Empire (A.D. 830–906), the most western of the Slav races enjoyed a period of glory. However, this was rudely shattered three-quarters of a century later by the invading Magyars. There was no hope of re-establishing the empire. Following their defeat in 955 by Otto I and his subsequent coronation as Holy Roman Emperor, the line of Bohemian kings was left with virtually no alternative other than to pay tribute to the elected successors of Otto: to the Saxons, the Salians, the Hohenstaufens and finally the Hapsburgs. After Christianity reached the Bohemian lands early in the ninth century, the racially minded Slavs resented the political pressure of the German missionaries and the linguistic pressure of those from Rome. Prince Rastislav (c. 863) invited the two Thessalonian missionaries, Methodius and his brother Constantine (later known as Cyril), to Moravia, knowing that they would preach in the Slav tongue instead of in Latin. They translated the liturgical books into Old Slavonic and disseminated translations of passages from the Scriptures. For a while the liturgy included some Byzantine music, but after the fall of the Moravian Empire the influence of Rome became much stronger. Very gradually some of the plain-song was replaced by newly-composed Czech melodies. The earliest surviving melody is the eleventh-century *Hospodine, pomiluj ny* (Lord, have mercy). The famous *St Wenceslas* plain-song probably comes from the end of the next century. *Buch všemohúcí* (God Almighty), from the beginning of the fourteenth century, is the earliest Czech melody extant that has a distinct rhythmic basis.[1]

In the early fifteenth century the leaders of the Hussite movement relied greatly on sacred song as a means of gaining popular support. Some of their melodies were original, but many were adapted from Gregorian plainsong or from secular and folk sources. The *Hymnal of Jistebnice* (*c.* 1420) contains seventy-seven of these songs. The most historic melody of all, *Kdož jste Boží bojovníci!* (Ye who are God's warriors!), was sung so fervently on the battlefield by the Taborite soldiers that it terrified their enemies. This melody was used by Smetana in *Tábor* and *Blaník* and also by Dvořák and Suk. The Protestant tradition of unison hymn singing in Bohemia and Moravia was given a fresh impetus in the sixteenth century by the Moravian (or Czech) Brethren. Many collections of hymns and psalms were published, the first being Bishop Luke of Prague's anthology of 1501. Jan Blahoslav, whose importance rests mainly on his translation of the New Testament into Czech (1565), issued his famous *Šamotulny Hymnal* in 1561. Almost a century later Bishop Comenius published the last important collection, the celebrated *Book of Psalms and Sacred Songs* (1659). Motets in up to five parts were composed early in the sixteenth century, but it was not until the time of Jan Trojan (Trojan Turnovský), Jiří Rychnovský and more especially Harant of Polžice (1564–1621) that works of real distinction were composed.

The Emperor Ferdinand I (1526–64) set an example to his successors and to leading aristocrats like the Rožmberks by establishing a fine orchestra at his court at Prague. He recognized the need for a minimum of religious freedom, and by signing the treaty of Augsburg (1555) secured peace for his empire for half a century. But when the horrors of the Thirty Years War were unleashed the dissident Czechs and Moravians were among the chief sufferers. Their humiliating defeat at the Battle of the White Mountain (1620) was followed by more than two centuries of domination by the Hapsburgs. Although musical life was seriously disrupted, Karel Lichtenstein of Kastelkorn, Prince-Bishop of Olomouc, was able to found a highly important

[1] Jan Racek's *Česká hudba* (1958) and *Československý hudební slovník* (1963–1965) have been helpful in the preparation of this chapter.

centre for the establishment of instrumental music at Kroměříž. P. J. Vejvanovský (d. 1693) composed serenatas, ballets and sacred music there, and the violinist Heinrich Biber (1644–1704) was there until he moved to Salzburg, where he composed the sacred drama *Wenzes-laus Bohemiae rex et martyr*. A. V. Michna (d. 1676), the leading Czech exponent of the baroque style, composed a *St Wenceslas Mass* for six solo voices, six-part choir and orchestra. At the end of the century a few operas were written to Italian librettos on episodes from Czech history and legend, the most favoured subject being the legendary founding of the first Bohemian dynasty. Much later Smetana based his festival opera *Libuše* on the same theme. At least one Italian com-poser chose the same subject for an opera. This was Bartolomeo Mernardi's *La Libusse*, sometimes claimed to be the first work for the stage on a Czech national theme; it had been preceded, however, some six years earlier by *Primislao, primo re di Boemia*, produced at Venice in 1698 and the work of an unknown composer. Long before this, Czech and Moravian folk-song had become absorbed into some of the hymns of the Hussites and Moravian Brethren. Folk-song had been used as *cantus firmi* by various composers, and Turnovský is believed to have written a four-part mass on the folk melody *Dunaj, voda hluboká*. It would be fruitless to attempt to recognize a clear-cut Czech style in the music of most of the composers of these times, but Michna and Zelenka (1679–1745) instilled elements of folk-song and something of its spirit into their music.

The political, economic, social and religious conditions that pre-vailed during the eighteenth century proved to be quite intolerable to musicians. In consequence during a span of a century most of the leading Czech composers migrated for one or more of these reasons to Vienna, Mannheim, Dresden, Berlin, Paris, London and numerous other cities. It is possible to offer at least a partial explanation for such a remarkable outpouring of talent. Owing to the severe nature of their oppression the people sought solace in music-making, which was therefore fostered to a far greater extent than ever before. The village schoolmaster was invariably a musician who taught his pupils to play the violin and to sing. The musicians who made names for them-selves were educated at Jesuit schools, where a sound musical training was provided. The thoroughness and efficiency of musical training in Bohemia and Moravia were proverbial, so that it became known as 'the conservatory of Europe'. But, above all, the flowering of Czech music at this time testifies to the profound musical instinct and feeling of the nation. The atmosphere in the princely courts in Germany was far more conducive to fine artistic work than the conditions at home. Great interest was shown in the French enlightenment, and close contact was made with leading figures in this new world of thought. Distinguished artists and musicians paid visits to the courts or were invited to become resident there. If musicians like the Bendas were seeking religious toleration, they had no difficulty in finding it. The Bendas's relations, the Brixis, preferred to remain at home. František Brixi (1732–71) was a distinguished choirmaster at St Vitus Cathedral, Prague, and Mozart's host František Xaver Dušek (1731–99), an outstanding pianist, teacher and composer, also had no desire to emigrate; but these men were almost unique at this time.

The Elector Palatine, Duke Carl Theodor, enlisted the services at his palace at Mannheim of the composer and theorist Franz Xaver Richter (1709–89), of the cellist and composer Anton Filtz, or Fils (c. 1730–60), and of the violinist, conductor and composer Johann Stamitz (1717–57). Besides forging the Duke's orchestra into an instrument of great precision, capable of performing with an unprecedented range of expression and dynamics, Stamitz was in the forefront of early symphonic composition and made an important contribution towards the evolution of sonata form. František Benda (1709–86), a violinist, was the first of his family to go to Germany. He served Crown Prince Frederick at Rheinsberg, and when his master became Frederick the Great he followed him to Potsdam. His young brother George, or Jiří (1722–95), became Duke Frederick III's Kapellmeister at Gotha, where he composed sonatas, symphonies, concertos, cantatas and *Singspiele*. However, his *Ariadne auf Naxos* and *Medea* (1775), dramatic works in which song is replaced by speech accompanied by music (i.e. melodrama), attracted even greater attention. Rousseau's *Pygmalion* had already paved the way, but Benda set an example to future Czech composers, such as Fibich. Mozart saw both works at Mannheim and commented: 'Never has anything surprised

4

KATEŘINA SMETANA IN 1858
Oil painting by J. P. Södermark

SMETANA IN 1858
Oil painting by J. P. Södermark

me so much. . . . . You know that Benda was always my favourite among the Lutheran Kapellmeisters.'

Many Czech musicians were drawn towards the court, opera houses, palaces and churches of Vienna. Fux's pupil František I. Tůma (1704–74) wrote church music and was the Empress Elisa﹣ beth's Kapellmeister, and Wenzel (Václav) Pichl (1741–1805) held a similar post under the Archduke Ferdinand. Leopold Koželuh (1747–1818) became court composer after Mozart, and was succeeded by František Krommer (1759–1831). Koželuh composed symphonies, piano music, operas and ballets. Florian Gassmann (1729–74) directed the *opera buffa* company at the Burg Theater, and Pavel and Antonín Vranický were leaders of the Imperial Opera orchestra. Pavel (Paul Wranitzky, 1756–1808), the elder brother, composed *Oberon, König der Elfen* (1789), a subject later used by Weber. Adalbert Gyrowetz, or Jírovec (1763–1850), wrote instrumental, stage and church music, and some of his symphonies were passed off as the work of Joseph Haydn. Perhaps the most gifted composer of this group was Jan K. Vaňhal, or Wanhal (1739–1813), who is remem﹣ bered for his hundred or so symphonies.

The virtuoso pianist and composer Jan Ladislav Dusík, or Dussek (1760–1812), celebrated for his piano concertos, travelled widely; he was employed by several princes and greatly admired by Marie﹣ Antoinette. Antonín Reicha (1770–1836) made Paris his home and is noted for his wind quintets, his theoretical works, and for having taught Berlioz, Liszt, Gounod and César Franck. He advocated the simultaneous use of eight differently tuned pairs of kettle drums. Mozart's friend Josef Mysliveček (1737–81), whom the Italians re﹣ named Venatorini and nick﹣named 'Il divino Boemo', had great success with his operas at Florence, Naples and Munich, whereas Jan Antonín Mareš (1719–94) became celebrated for his pioneer work as director of the Russian Count Naryshkin's horn band.

Only rarely did Czech composers set texts in the Czech language. F. X. Brixi almost always set Latin words, Mysliveček's operas are in Italian, P. Vranický's operas and Benda's *Singspiele* and melodramas are in German, and Reicha's operas are in French. Among the few works with Czech texts are the *50th Psalm* by František Adam J.

Miča (1746–1811) and Koželuh's *Masonic Songs*, published in Berlin, *c.* 1800. Towards the close of the eighteenth century Czech writers and scholars were strongly influenced by Rousseau's plea for self-expres-sion, by Herder's belief that the poetry of any nation must embody traditional and environmental features characteristic of the race with-out being affected by alien influences, and also by the spirit of revolt that culminated in the French Revolution. But since the German language was so deeply entrenched, a prolonged and bitter struggle was necessary before the Czech language could achieve supremacy. Interest was at first centred on the Czech tongue and related Slavonic languages and on the history of Bohemia, and in both fields the scientific work of Josef Dobrovský (1753–1829) was of vital impor-tance. Václav Thám's *Poems in Verse Speech* (1785), an anthology of old and new poems, was the first book of Czech verse to be pub-lished. The *Dvůr Králové* (Queen's Court) manuscript, which Vácslav Hanka (1791–1861), the poet and philologist, claimed to have dis-covered in 1817, made a deep impression and was accepted as genuine by most people, although Dobrovský was sceptical about its authen-ticity. The opening of the Estates Theatre (1783), the inauguration of the first Czech newspaper (1786) and the founding of the Chair of Czech Language and Literature at Charles University, Prague (1793), were signs of the growing strength of the literary movement.

Despite the difficulties of publishing music in a language that was not officially recognized, Jakob Jan Ryba (1765–1815) succeeded in issuing a set of songs in 1800, and his example was followed twelve years later by J. E. Doležálek (1780–1858). Václav Jan Tomášek (1774–1850) published settings of poems by Hanka, V. Nejedlý and Marek as *Six Songs*, Op. 48, in 1813, and a further set of Hanka songs ten years later. An important two-volume collection of *Czech Songs*, which contained compositions by František Škroup (1801–62) and some minor figures and was edited by Simeon Macháček, appeared in 1825. Since Tomášek published *Six Eclogues*, Op. 35, in 1807, seven years before the earliest of Field's *Nocturnes*, he is credited with being the initiator of the nineteenth-century 'mood piece'. He followed these with a set of Rhapsodies and several more sets of Eclogues, and in 1818 published *Three Dithyrambs*, Op. 65.

Jan Václav (Hugo) Voříšek, or Woržischek (1791–1825), followed his teacher Tomášek's example by publishing as his Op. 1 a set of *Twelve Rhapsodies* (1818). His *Impromptus*, Op. 7, appeared in 1822, five years before Schubert's similarly named pieces and more than a year before the *Moments musicaux*. His Symphony in D combines an almost Beethovenian forcefulness and directness with a romantic sensibility and a little Czech colouring.

Possibly the first opera performance in Czech took place at Jaroměřice Castle in December 1730, when a translated version of *L'origine di Jaromeritz in Moravia* by František Václav Miča (1694–1744) was presented. Miča wrote other operas, now lost, which may also have been sung in his native tongue. We hear no more of opera in Czech until an enterprising Italian troupe sang *The Magic Flute* (*c.* 1794) and Paisiello's *Nina* (1796) in Prague in Czech translations.[1] J. N. Štěpánek (1783–1844) provided translations of Mozart's *Die Entführung* (1806) and Dalayrac's *Deux mots* (1815), and in 1823 Macháček helped to inaugurate a new era in his country's operatic history with his translation of J. Weigl's popular success *Die Schweitzerfamilie*. At this time French and Italian operas were sung in German in Prague, but within the next two years Štěpánek, Macháček, Chmelenský and Doucha provided translations of *Der Freischütz*, *Don Giovanni*, Cherubini's *Water Carrier*, Rossini's *Barber of Seville* and *Otello*, Méhul's *Joseph* and Rossini's *Tancredi*. Many other works followed.

The real turning point came on 2nd February 1826 when František Škroup's simple and melodious *Singspiel*-type opera *Dráteník* (The Tinker) with a libretto by Chmelenský was performed at the Estates Theatre. This is the first opera known for certain to have been composed to a Czech text. He followed this with two other Czech operas, *Oldřich a Božena* (1828) and *Libušin sňatek* (Libuše's Wedding, 1835), but lack of success forced him to turn to German librettos. The Czech national anthem, *Kde domov můj?* (Where is my home?) comes from Škroup's incidental music to J. K. Tyl's farce *Fidlovačka*. *Žižka's Oak*, an opera on a Hussite subject by František B. Kott (1808–84) was

---

[1] Loewenberg, *Annals of Opera*, 1943.

mounted in German at Brno in 1841 and a year later in a Czech translation. His second opera *Dalibor*, with which he anticipated Smetana, is not known to have been performed. *Žižka's Oak* reappeared in Prague in 1847 after Jiří Macourek (1815 to after 1863) made a new setting of the Czech libretto. Although Škroup's brother Jan Nepomuk Škroup (1811–92) composed *The Swedes in Prague* in 1845, he failed to have it produced until 1867.

Musically speaking the foundations that were laid by F. Škroup and his contemporaries were very insubstantial, and it would be absurd to compare their meagre achievements with those of the leading composers in other countries. But if Škroup succeeded in arousing some interest in his work, he was justified in his uphill struggle to create an indigenous school of opera, one that was more characteristically Czech in spirit than anything we may find in the work of Mysliveček, George Benda, Pavel Vranický, Gyrowetz and Reicha. He can at least be said to have made the path of Smetana a shade easier.

CHAPTER II

THE COMPOSER'S ANCESTRY AND YOUTH

Bedřich Smetana's ancestors may be traced back as far as the four-teenth century. The various branches of the family lived in north-east Bohemia, and especially in the area between Nový Bydžov (to the west of Hradec Králové) and Česká Skalice, and at Nové Město nad Metují. These places lie in a most attractive region close to the Silesian border and nestling under the northern end of the Orlické Hory (Eagle Mountains). Smetana's great-great-great-grandfather, Petr Smetana (c. 1625–25th February 1687), was a highly respected man whom Count Johann A. Schaffgotsch consulted about local affairs. When the Count made Nechanice his principal seat, Petr became a magistrate there, a post he held from 1665 to 1681.[1] Petr's second son Václav Smetana (c. 1650–1728) married Ludmila Strunová on 2nd June 1678, and eight of their children survived infancy. The Schaff-gotsch family still relied on the service of members of the Smetana family, for we find that Václav's eldest son Jan was the cooper at the brewery attached to the château at Sádová, and that his younger brother Matěj (22nd February 1683–4th April 1742), who became Smetana's great-grandfather, was gardener of the château park. Matěj had four children by his first wife and five by his second wife, Johanna. Her second child, born on 17th January 1730 and named Václav after his grandfather, was Smetana's paternal grandfather. He became the Count's cooper at Sádová and married Ludmila Konárovská, the daughter of a wood carver, on 21st January 1758. Their eleven children included four sons, and of these Josef took charge of the gardens at Sviništ'ana château, Václav was cooper to the lord of Hořice and František was a brewer.

František Smetana, the composer's father, was born on 26th October

[1] Z. Nejedlý's *Bedřich Smetana*, vol. i, 2nd edn (1950), is an invaluable source of information on Smetana's ancestors.

1777. In many ways he was a remarkable man, since he had a good head for business and was more enterprising than his forbears, a factor that led him to move from place to place and away from the area where his ancestors lived and worked. In early life he spent some time in Lower Austria and at Dobřan, near Pilsen. He married Anna Bartoníčková, the orphaned daughter of a soap manufacturer with a little property of her own, early in April 1806, after being appointed assistant at the brewery at Česká Skalice. Soon afterwards they moved to Nysa in Silesia, where František leased a brewery. He did a roaring trade with Napoleon's troops stationed there and put aside at least 100,000 zlotys. He returned to Česká Skalice, and at about the same time his wife died in childbirth and their daughter failed to live. He next settled at Chalkovice where he again leased a brewery, and on 30th July 1809 married Ludmila Exnerová, the orphaned daughter of a highly cultured Jaroměř family. Her father had been Mayor of Jaroměř for ten years and had represented his town at the coronation of Leopold II in 1791. Two of their first children, a daughter and a son, failed to live, but four daughters survived: Anna (b. 1811), Klára (b. 1815), Žofie (b. 1816) and Marie (b. 1818). When the brewery lease expired in 1818 František left Chalkovice for Nové Město nad Metují, where he took charge of Prince Franz Josef Dietrichstein's extremely well-equipped brewery. But Ludmila's health was deteriorating, and on 13th September 1820 she died, three and a half months after giving birth to a daughter who was named after her.

Ten weeks later, on 20th November, František married for the third time. His bride, twenty-nine-year-old Barbora Lynková, came from a family of millers, although her father, Jan Lynek, was an official at Poličan. Her maternal grandfather had been Count Morzin's postilion. After the newly wedded couple settled down at Nové Město, František must have been disappointed to see Barbora following the example of her predecessors and adding to the number of daughters in the family, first with Albina (b. 1821) and then Františka (b. 1823), for he was relying on her to give him a son and heir. In the autumn of 1823 František moved forty miles farther south to Litomyšl to take an even better position as brewer to Count Waldstein. The Count's splendid Renaissance castle dominates this attractive little town. Their youngest daughter died just after they arrived there. Like her husband, Barbora was extremely fond of dancing, and on the Monday before Lent she danced until almost midnight. A few hours later, on Shrove Tuesday, 2nd March 1824 at 10 a.m., she gave her husband what he most ardently desired, a son. According to the account that the future composer's sisters gave of Bedřich Smetana's birth, a maidservant brought the wonderful news to František when he was in the castle courtyard, and he was so overjoyed that he immediately seized the girl and danced with her.[1] He then called for a barrel of beer to be brought to the courtyard so that all the servants could join in the celebration.[2]

František had learnt to play the violin when quite young and he was an enthusiastic player in later years, especially while he was at Chalkovice, where he often played violin duets by Pleyel and Gyrowetz with his friend František Černý. Barbora does not appear to have been particularly musical, so we may assume that it was from his father that Bedřich inherited most of his musical talent. Nejedlý summed up the composer's indebtedness to his parents in this way: 'His ardour and passionate affection for all those who were loyal to him were certainly inherited first of all from his mother and her family, just as his energy, courage, persistence and capacity for work were primarily derived from his father.'[3]

František was extremely proud of his son, and no doubt the family made a fuss of him and tended to spoil him a little. František lost no opportunity to find out if Bedřich was musical, and he gave him some elementary musical instruction when he was barely four years old. In the brief autobiography at the beginning of Bedřich's first diary, written when he was sixteen, he says his father taught him about musical time,[4] but he also learnt the violin and made rapid progress, for we are told that when he was only five he was able to lead a Haydn string quartet on his father's name-day.[5] Possibly he only played first violin

---

[1] K. Teige, *Kalendář českých hudebníků* (1891).

[2] A. Hnilička, 'Friedrich Smetana's Jugendjahre', *Union*, no. 104.

[3] Nejedlý, *op. cit.*, vol. i, p. 326.

[4] Literally 'the musical bar'. Nejedlý, *op. cit.*, vol. ii, p. 143.

[5] E. Meliš, biography in *Dalibor*, vol. v (1863), p. 185; also Rieger's *Naučný slovník*, vol. viii (1870), p. 690.

in selected movements. He started attending the Piarist School at five and a half years of age and probably at the same time began having piano and violin lessons from a local musician named Jan Chmelík (1777–1849). Chmelík and his father must certainly have introduced him to the French operatic music that was popular at that time. Much later Bedřich recalled having improvised at Litomyšl, and that Chmelík wrote down for him his first compositions, a waltz and a galop.[1] His progress as a pianist was phenomenal, and when only six and a half he performed a piano arrangement of Auber's *La Muette de Portici* (*Masaniello*) overture at a concert of the local Philosophical Academy on the name-day of Emperor Franz II, 4th October 1830. In later years this was a happy memory which he commemorated with a jubilee concert.

The birth in 1825 of Barbora's second son Antonín, which brought the number of living children up to eight, intensified the need for the family to move to more spacious quarters. They went to a fine house in the square of Litomyšl, which later became the town hall. Two more children were born, Barbora in 1827 and Karel in 1830, and two others died when only a few months old. The household was completed by Barbora's parents and her brother Josef. Early in 1831 František left Litomyšl for an even better position at Jindřichův Hradec in southern Bohemia, where he signed a four-year contract to rent Count Johann Rudolf Czernin's brewery. This was a larger town and a more important cultural centre than Litomyšl. The magnificent castle, dating from the thirteenth century, was rebuilt in the sixteenth century and included a theatre. Count Czernin was a keen violinist and patron of the arts, and was Intendant of the Imperial Theatre in Vienna from 1828. He owned a piano that had been played on by Mozart, whom he knew personally and greatly admired,[2]

---

[1] E. Krásnohorská, *Bedřich Smetana* (1885), p. 3.

[2] Count Czernin von Chudenitz (1756–1845), described by Mozart as 'but a young puppy', was a nephew of Count Hieronymus Collorado, Archbishop of Salzburg. His father, Count Prokop Adalbert Czernin, settled an annual sum of twenty ducats on Mozart, but died a year later, probably without having received the first of the expected compositions.

and his enthusiasm for Mozart had a marked effect on the impressionable Bedřich.

For two years Bedřich attended the elementary school in the town, and his marks for Religious Knowledge and reading and writing German and Latin were good. His behaviour was exemplary, and in recognition of his good work his name was inscribed in the 'Golden Book'. In view of his excellent progress he was transferred to the grammar school when he was only nine years old. His studies at the new school ended prematurely, not because of unsatisfactory work or conduct, but for some unexplained reason.[1] The local organist and choirmaster, František Ikavec (1801–60), gave him violin and piano lessons and found him a useful member of the choir, where he sang the soprano solos. Bedřich's earliest surviving composition, a Galop in D major thirtytwo bars long, written in his own handwriting, originated during this time but cannot be dated exactly.[2] After losing another baby girl, František and Barbora's family was completed by the birth of another daughter Františka in 1833. The Smetanas were particularly friendly with the family of Karel Kolář, a commissioner of taxes with a musical wife. Bedřich was on excellent terms with their eldest son Karel and Bedřich's sister Barbora was very friendly with Kateřina.

In 1835 at the age of fiftyseven František paid 21,050 zlotys for an estate at Růžkovy Lhotice, near Čechtice and the historic Blaník Mountain in southeast Bohemia, and retired there. In this pleasant part of the country there were no good schools, so Bedřich and Antonín were sent to the grammar school at Jihlava (Iglau) thirty miles away, where they lodged with a tailor's family. From a musical point of view Jihlava was quite important, for its opera was even better than that at Brno. Victorin Maťocha (1801–62), who was a very able violinist and ran the thriving Music Society, became Bedřich's teacher. But the elevenyearold boy was far from happy in this big and predominantly German town, and was made even more

---

[1] Nejedlý, *op. cit.*, vol. ii, pp. 385–8, 404.

[2] The date on the manuscript, '832', was added by the composer at a later date and may not be reliable. Facsimile in Nejedlý, *op. cit.*, vol. ii.

miserable by Antonín Svoboda, the tailor, who is reputed to have been a martinet.[1] He did very badly in the second class at school and made little progress.[2] His father was therefore compelled to make fresh plans for him. He tried to get him admitted in the middle of the school year to the grammar school at Německý Brod (now Havlíčkův Brod), but his bad report made this impossible.

Both boys went to the new school in the autumn of 1836. The grammar school at Německý Brod was founded by the Augustinian order and taken over later by the Premonstratensians. It was roughly half the size of the school at Jihlava. Because of the setback in his academic progress, Bedřich was placed in the lowest class like his brother. His work proceeded smoothly, and in three years he passed satisfactorily through the first three classes. He liked the liberal-minded atmosphere of the town, and was delighted that Father Karel Šindelář, who taught grammar and humanities, was an ardent music lover. Bedřich had no music lessons at Německý Brod, but he often visited Šindelář, who showed him his vocal score of Hérold's *Zampa* and frequently asked the young boy to play a favourite work of his, the *Freischütz* overture. Bedřich became very friendly with two of his schoolfellows, Karel Havlíček (b. 1821), who wrote German poems, later adopted the name of Borovský and became a revolutionary patriot, and František Butula (b. 1820), who was a singer and quite a capable cellist. He missed them when they left for Prague in 1838. At that time the city was a highly important centre of political, social and cultural thought, and acted as a powerful magnet on young people with lively minds and philosophical and artistic leanings. A fairly wide repertory of operas was performed at the German opera house and there were occasional visits from Europe's most famous musicians.

Bedřich soon made up his mind that he too must taste what Prague had to offer; fortunately his father was most co-operative. By pulling

[1] V. V. Zelený in *K životopisu B. Smetany* (1884), p. 13, states that the unhappy boy wept for three days and nights.

[2] His report for the first term of 1836 gave him a good mark for conduct, satisfactory marks in Religion, History and Geography, but his Latin, Mathematics and application were unsatisfactory. Nejedlý, *op. cit.*, vol. iii, p. 59.

some strings he arranged for him to attend the fourth class of the Academic Grammar School in the capital, which was directed by Josef Jungmann, the distinguished philologist and active leader of the movement for national revival. Liszt gave five concerts in Prague in March 1840, a few months after Bedřich arrived there, and included in his programmes a Beethoven Sonata in C minor (Op. 13?) and movements from the *Pastoral* symphony, his own Fantasia on Bellini's *I Puritani* and transcriptions of Schubert's *Erlkönig*, *Serenade* and *Ave Maria* and of the overture to *William Tell*, various compositions of his own, concert pieces of Weber, and the *Hexameron* written by Chopin, Pixis, Thalberg, Czerny, Herz and most notably by Liszt himself. In his diary the youth noted that these were 'Sehr schöne Tage'.[1] For some weeks Bedřich had been so carried away by the delights of Prague that he had played truant from school. When František arrived in the city in May and inquired about his son's progress he was greatly upset by what Jungmann told him. But Bedřich was not immediately packed off home, as is sometimes thought, for his diary makes it clear that he visited an uncle at Nové Město in the second half of June and did not leave Prague finally until about 10th July 1840.[2]

In the autumn he went to stay with his cousin, Professor František Smetana (1801–61), at Pilsen, so that he could go to the Premonstratensian grammar school there. He started in the fourth class, and remained at the school until he matriculated in 1843. Being an exceptionally gifted pianist, he was in great demand for social events in the more prosperous Pilsen homes, where dancing was the main diversion. He had a great zest for dancing, and since the Kolář family had moved to Pilsen he was often able to have Kateřina, a friend of earlier days, as his dancing partner. He was captivated by this charming girl, who was also an excellent pianist, but his constant attentions were an embarrassment to her.

Bedřich had had no systematic musical training since the age of twelve, but he often felt the urge to compose. When in Prague he

[1] Nejedlý, *op. cit.*, vol. v, pp. 332–4, 464–5.
[2] Nejedlý, *op. cit.*, vol. v, pp. 464–7. J. Neruda's account, which appears in F. Bartoš's *Bedřich Smetana, Letters and Reminiscences*, is untrustworthy.

wrote pieces for his quartet with Butula, František Kostka and Vilém Vlček, including an overture in the style of Mozart. He thought little of some of these works, but particularly liked a Polka written for his cousin Louise at Nové Město (1840), a Grand Polka in B flat for Ludmila Pradáčová (1841) and *From a Student's Life*, a Polka in C of a year later. In 1842 he wrote an Overture in C minor for piano duet for Kateřina's name-day, and a Minuet and *Galop Bajaderek* for large orchestra. [1] As his schooldays drew towards their close it became abundantly clear that the only profession that would satisfy Bedřich was music. He recorded his ambition in his diary for 23rd January 1845 as follows: 'By the Grace of God and with his help I shall one day be a Liszt in technique and a Mozart in composition.'

[1] The youthful compositions are published in *Edice Souborná díla B. Smetany I, Skladby z mládí do r. 1843* (1924). A complete list of the early compositions appears in Nejedlý, *op. cit.*, vol. vii.

CHAPTER III

YEARS OF STRUGGLE

When František found that his son was determined to take up a musical career he gave his consent, but warned him that his path would be fraught with difficulty. František was in a far less favourable financial position than formerly, for he was losing money in endeavouring to maintain Růžkovy Lhotice, and was obliged to sell it and return to the brewing trade. He resumed his former work at Obříství, near Mělník. It was impossible to support Bedřich, so he gave him twenty gulden towards his first expenses in Prague. The nineteen-year-old youth shared a room with two law students at the home of his Aunt Pepi (Josephine). He was too old to enter the Conservatory, could not afford to have private lessons and was unable either to hire or borrow a piano. Soon his position became desperate. Kateřina Kolářová was already studying music and lodging with the blind pianist and pedagogue Josef Proksch (1794–1864), who founded his school of music in Prague in 1830. But since Bedřich had not been introduced to Proksch and was also penniless, he was unable to call at the house. Besides this, Kateřina was in no mood to see him. When at last he succeeded in hiring a piano for six gulden a month at the beginning of December, he spent all his time practising. The last entry in the diary of his youth continues the story: [1]

My Katie's mother paid me a surprise visit one day, and seeing that my affairs were in a deplorable state insisted that I went with her to Proksch in the hope that he could offer me some teaching. I went with her, played several studies to him as well as I knew how, and awaited his verdict. He praised my touch, nothing else, and after having asked about my previous

---

[1] Summary of the previous years, dated 16th August 1847. Bartoš, *op. cit.*; German text in E. Rychnovsky, *Smetana* (1924), pp. 45–6.

musical instruction and heard my excessively naïve views on my future theoretical education by means of self-tuition, at which he smiled disapprovingly, he called in Jan Richter, one of his best pupils, to play to me. Whether this was to put me to shame or to be a lesson to me I can't be sure. Although the young man possessed a far more polished technique than I his performance left me cold; I was even reassured, without deceiving myself, regarding my own worth. Katie, however, hardly seemed to notice me. Finally Katie's mother asked Proksch to take me on as a pupil in Theory, which he agreed to do after much persuasion, solely as he said because of my talent, and at a fee of one gulden a lesson. Although I realized I wasn't in a position to pay him this fee, I was glad nevertheless to obtain instruction in the Theory of Music, which had been a closed book to me until then; and without worrying in the least how I could pay him I placed myself entirely in the hands of the Almighty.

Fortunately for Bedřich the director of the Conservatory, Jan B. Kittl (1809–68), heard of his plight, no doubt through Proskch. Kittl then arranged for the young musician to call on Count Leopold F. Thun, who needed a resident piano teacher for his large family. Smetana accepted the post at a salary of three hundred gulden per annum and commenced his duties on 18th January 1844. He remained a member of the Thun household until 1st June 1847. He was treated as one of the family, and soon found that Elisabeth von Thun was the only one with a spark of music. With this security and enough free time to pursue his composition exercises, especially when he went with the family to their hunting lodge 'Bon Repos' or to Poběžovice in the Bohemian Forest, he made rapid strides in his work for Proksch. The two-, three- and four-part fugues, the canons, movements in sonata form and rondo form, a Sonata in G minor, sets of variations, studies and numerous miscellaneous pieces composed during the years 1845–6 provide ample evidence of Bedřich's strong determination to make good the serious deficiencies of his earlier musical training.

Several events occurred during this period that were bound to stimulate a budding composer with a lively interest in contemporary music. Berlioz gave three concerts in Prague in mid January 1846, conducting among other things his *King Lear* overture and the *Symphonie fantastique*, a work that made a powerful impression on the young man. Berlioz returned to Prague at the end of March to present *Romeo and Juliet*, and when Proksch held a soirée in his honour on 10th April Smetana was almost certainly present, and if so was undoubtedly introduced to him. Liszt revisited Prague at about the same time. In the following January Count Thun entertained Robert and Clara Schumann at his palace, and Smetana showed them one of his compositions. They detected the influence of Berlioz, and Clara made an unfavourable comment about this in her diary.

Having finished his studies with Proksch at the age of twenty-three, Smetana decided first to make himself known as a piano virtuoso and then to found his own music school. He arranged for Kateřina to become the piano teacher in the Thun family, and then set about planning a series of recitals in the towns and spas of north-west Bohemia. The programme of the first concert, at Cheb (Eger) on 7th August 1847, points clearly in the direction of some of the composers he admired: the variations from Beethoven's Sonata in A flat (Op. 26), two studies by Chopin, some of Mendelssohn's *Songs Without Words*, Schubert's *Serenade* arranged by Liszt, and some Czech melodies arranged by himself. But the concert was so poorly attended that he abandoned the rest of the tour. Following this fiasco he seized the chance of taking part in Jan Hoffmann's Chamber Subscription Concerts in Prague, and after having played in Onslow's Sextet, Op. 30, on 12th December the critic of *Bohemia* commended him for his technique, taste and understanding. The programme on 7th January comprised Kalkbrenner's Septet, Op. 32, Beethoven's Wind Quintet, Op. 16, and Schubert's Piano Trio in E flat, and this time Smetana appeared in every item.

Smetana's relationship with Kateřina had improved greatly, but it was essential to augment the twelve gulden a month that his teaching brought in before he could contemplate marriage. On 28th January 1848 he applied for permission to open a music school, and, greatly daring, he wrote to Liszt on 23rd March, explaining his difficulties and dramatizing them a little, asking Liszt to accept his *Six Characteristic Pieces*, Op. 1, and find a publisher for them, and finally begging him to lend him four hundred gulden. Liszt replied as follows, but ignored the request for a loan:[1]

> The *Morceaux Caractéristiques* together with the accompanying letter were handed to me barely a quarter of an hour before my departure for Vienna. First of all I should like to express my warm thanks for the dedication, which I accept with all the more pleasure since the pieces are the most outstanding, finely felt and most polished that have come to my notice recently. . . . Even though it is difficult to find a good publisher today for a good work unless it is signed by a name that is well-known and will sell, I hope nevertheless to be able to give you news soon about the publication of your *Morceaux Caractéristiques*, and I shall certainly do what I can to see that you receive a satisfactory fee, which should encourage you to establish active contact with the publisher.
>
> If my way should lead through Prague this summer, as seems likely, I should be very pleased to call on you to thank you personally.

Even though the pieces were not published by Franz Kistner until three years later and no fee was paid, this response was an encouragement and proved to be the beginning of a friendship that was greatly valued by Smetana. He heard in May that he could go ahead with the music school, and on 8th August, without the help of Liszt, he opened his school at his modest apartment in the Old Town Square.

We may be sure that Professor F. J. Smetana of Pilsen aired his patriotic views in Bedřich's hearing during the years 1840–3. When the young musician was planning his ill-fated concert tour, his uncle wrote very frankly, saying:[2] 'If you, a Slav by birth and nationality, should travel as a German virtuoso, even though you are showered with honours, you would be renouncing national recognition, which is more valuable than gold.' Karel Havlíček and other radically minded friends would have attempted to instil similar ideas into Smetana's mind, yet he is not known to have had pronounced national feelings much before the Revolution of 1848, and even later there were periods when political matters were not dominant in his mind.

---

[1] Smetana's letter and Liszt's reply (30th March) appear in Rychnovsky, *op. cit.*, pp. 54–7.

[2] Letter of 10th July 1847. Bartoš, *op. cit.*

But the meteoric rise of Kossuth in Hungary and fall of Metternich in Vienna focused attention on the fatal weaknesses and racial injustices of the Austrian autocratic system, so that when the Revolution broke out in Prague on 11th June 1848, Smetana could no longer stand aside. He joined the Svornost (Concord) Corps and helped to man the barricades, until Prince von Windischgrätz crushed the revolt. Stirred by the excitement of those days he composed a *March of the Prague Students' Legion*, a *March of the National Guard*, a unison *Song of Freedom* to words by J. J. Kolár, and his first symphonic work, the festive Overture in D. Even though his parents understood Czech and the servants spoke it, Smetana was brought up to speak German, and it was a long time before he realized how important it was for him to master his own language. Probably the political events of 1848 made him aware of this shortcoming, but he was slow to remedy the deficiency, and did not attempt to write a letter in Czech until more than eight years later.[1]

Smetana's music school brought in very little income, but he was able to augment this by taking members of the Thun and Nostitz families as private pupils and by paying regular visits to Prague Castle to play with and to the deposed, imbecile Emperor Ferdinand. As his affairs were beginning to show some stability, he and Kateřina were married on 27th August 1849. During the next few years the couple was blissfully happy. Their first daughter Bedřiška (Frederica) was born on 7th January 1851 and two more daughters followed, Gabriela Jelčinka and Žofie, on 26th February 1852 and 24th May 1853. During this period Smetana wrote many piano pieces, and took a special interest in romantic mood pieces and polkas for the salon rather than for dancing.

The Czechs looked forward to the time when the young Emperor Franz Josef would be crowned King of Bohemia. His marriage with Elisabeth of Bavaria on 24th April 1854 led to hopes of greater understanding by him of the Czechs' desire for equality with the other nationalities within the empire, and in view of this he was

[1] Letter written on 23rd December 1856 to his parents, sent from Göteborg. The language is decidedly stilted.

supported by František Palacký, Karel Havlíček Borovský and other ardent patriots. Smetana wrote a *Triumphal Symphony* to commemorate the wedding, quoting the Emperor's Hymn, as he had already done in his *March of the National Guard*, but when he asked if he might dedicate the new work to the Emperor he received no response.

It was shortly after this that a series of misfortunes began to strike Smetana and his wife. First, two-year-old Gabriela developed tuberculosis and died on 9th July 1854. Next, to her father's intense sorrow, Bedřiška contracted scarlet fever and died on 6th September in the following year. Even though she was hardly more than four years old, she was already showing signs of having exceptional musical gifts. Smetana wrote his Piano Trio in G minor in memory of her. A fourth daughter, Kateřina, was born on 25th October 1855, but she survived only until 10th June. These tragedies were undermining the health of Smetana's wife, who was already known to be suffering from tuberculosis.

<small>First Page of Smetana's Letter to Dr L. Procházka</small>
Dated 11th March 1860 and written in Czech

CHAPTER IV

After the Revolution those who lived in the outer regions of the empire saw their hopes of greater liberty whittled away. The democratic constitutions of Kroměříž and Stadion were jettisoned. Franz Josef made it clear that he would not allow any advisory council to interfere with his absolute power, and then arranged for his empire to be administered as a single unit by the autocratic Alexander Bach. Czech patriots became more and more dispirited as they saw the tide of radicalism and liberalism stemmed. Smetana was disappointed over the turn of political events, but he also had personal problems and worries. It was burdensome and not particularly remunerative to run a music school, and his heart was not in his teaching unless his pupils were gifted or attractive, and preferably both. Kateřina's malady was a perpetual source of anxiety to him. It was unfortunate too that he chose to perform his *Triumphal Symphony* on 26th February 1855, because on that day there was a postponed performance of *Tannhäuser*, which diminished his audience seriously. Those who were there appreciated the scherzo most.

About a year later Alexander Dreyschock, the piano virtuoso for whom Smetana had written his *Allegro capriccioso*, returned from Scandinavia with glowing accounts of his successful concert tour of Sweden. He told Smetana that Mrs Eleonore Dickson, the wife of a rich Göteborg merchant, had asked him to look out for a piano teacher who might be willing to settle in that city. Smetana bore this in mind, but was not prepared to take any precipitate action. When Liszt was in Prague at the end of September to conduct his *Estergom* (Gran) *Mass*, Smetana had long conversations with him far into the night, and doubtless they discussed the younger man's future prospects as well as the aims and ideals of the progressive composer. After this Smetana quickly made up his mind to try his luck at Göteborg; he departed for Sweden on 11th October and arrived at his destination five days later. Losing no time over introducing himself to the public, he gave a recital on the 23rd and followed this with another concert on 12th November. On that date he was joined in Mendelssohn's D minor Trio by Josef Czapek, the Czech violinist who conducted the Harmoniska Sällskapet (Harmonic Society) orchestra, and August Meissner, a German cellist and conductor who was also resident at Göteborg. He opened a music school on 1st December, and also became conductor of the Society for Classical Choral Music. When the choral section of Harmoniska Sällskapet merged with this society a year later, Smetana conducted the enlarged choir.[1]

Smetana was so pleased to find his prospects were better than at home that he seriously considered the possibility of remaining permanently in Göteborg. So many ladies wished to take lessons from him that he found it impossible to cope with the demand. But even so he was less well off than he anticipated because he found it expensive living in Sweden, he had a home in Prague to maintain while he lived in an hotel in Göteborg, and he was trying to pay off a loan to his father. Before long he became aware of his musical isolation and it became apparent that permanent residence in Sweden was out of the question. In a letter to Liszt he was characteristically frank about the position in the prosperous city. 'The people here,' he wrote, 'are still firmly corroded within an antediluvian conception of art. Mozart is their idol, yet they don't even understand him. Beethoven frightens them, Mendelssohn is distasteful to them and they know nothing of the new men. I have introduced Schumann's work here for the first time.'[2] Nevertheless this situation provided him with the chance of doing valuable missionary work.

[1] Clara Thörnqvist, *Smetana in Goteborg, 1856–1862* (Göteborg, 1967) Dr Thörnqvist kindly informs me that the Harmoniska Sällskapet committee agreed on 15th October 1857 to ask the Society for Classical Choral Music to allow them to merge, that the latter gave their approval on 9th November 1857 and that their union was formally ratified by the Harmoniska Sällskapet on the 16th. The Choral Society was also known as the Society for Practising Vocal Music on Monday.

[2] Letter of 10th April 1857. Rychnovsky, *op. cit.*, pp. 69–70.

He organized a series of subscription chamber concerts to take place on 31st January and on 7th and 28th February 1857, with Czapek and Meissner as regular performers. Beethoven's *Ghost* Trio was played at the second concert, and the *Archduke* Trio and Schumann's Piano Quartet at the third. Each programme included a work by Mendelssohn. Long and arduous preparation was necessary for his performance of the first part of *Elijah* on 16th March, but the concert was most successful. At Smetana's concert on 18th April he played Beethoven's C minor Piano Concerto and conducted the Choral Society in Gade's *Elf King's Daughter*. He also appeared as soloist in some concerts arranged by others.

He made many friends and had a gay social life in Göteborg, but much the most significant and long-lasting friendship was with Mrs Fröjda Benecke, a twenty-year-old niece of the Jewish singing teacher A. Nissen. There was a very strong mutual attraction between Bedřich and Fröjda, and undoubtedly their intimacy did much to alleviate the composer's feelings of nostalgia during his voluntary exile. When revising his Polka in C in 1858 he renamed it *Vision at the Ball* and incorporated into it the series of notes FEDA, which suggests her name.

Soon after Smetana's return to Prague in the early summer of 1857 he was called to Nové Město nad Metují, where his father died on 12th June in his eightieth year. When Bedřich returned to Sweden twelve weeks later he took with him his wife Kateřina and their daughter Žofie. They stopped for four days at Weimar so that Smetana could see Liszt and attend the first performance of the *Faust* symphony and *Die Ideale*. It is probable that it was during this visit that Johann Herbeck humiliated the unfortunate Czech composer. The Viennese conductor taunted Smetana with being one of a race that had produced excellent fiddlers but not a single composer capable of writing a genuinely Czech work original enough to enrich European music. Smetana was unable to give a convincing reply. Liszt, however, came to his rescue by playing the *Six Characteristic Pieces* to the assembled company, declaring: 'Here is a composer with a genuine Czech heart, an artist by the Grace of God!' V. J. Novotný, who was one of the guests, asserted that on leaving Smetana solemnly swore to dedicate his entire life to his nation in the service of his art.[1] We cannot be certain that Smetana was convinced that it lay within his power to raise Czech music to a level comparable with that of other countries, but it is evident that he was determined to strive towards that end.

During his second season in Göteborg he opened a ladies' singing school and again ran a series of chamber concerts, at the second of which (11th February 1858) he performed his Pianoforte Trio. He was the soloist in Mozart's D minor concerto at Czapek's concert on 5th December and conducted choruses from Mendelssohn's *St Paul* at the violinist's concert on 2nd April. Schumann's *Paradise and the Peri* had been rehearsed during the previous season, and may have been sung at a Harmoniska Sällskapet soirée. Smetana's interest in Wagner was growing rapidly, and consequently he included choruses from *Tannhäuser* and *Lohengrin* in his programme of 14th April. He was gratified to find his audiences welcoming the newer works and asking for them to be repeated. His profound admiration for Liszt led to the composition of his first symphonic poem, *Richard III*, between April and July 1858.

Instead of returning home that summer the three Smetanas remained in Sweden. Bedřich did what he could to improve Kateřina's health by taking her for trips into the country and for a period to the spa of Särö, but there was no improvement at all and she dreaded the long Swedish winter that lay ahead. It became obvious that he would have to take her home at the first good opportunity, but in the meantime he became involved once more in the busy winter season of teaching and concerts, and in the composition of his second symphonic poem, *Wallenstein's Camp*. He increased the number of chamber concerts to six and then arranged three farewell concerts. In the second of these, a Harmoniska Sällskapet soirée on 23rd March, pupils of the singing school sang the terzetto from *William Tell* and the Furies chorus from Gluck's *Orfeo*.[2] In a letter to his mother-in-law he blamed himself for moving to a northern climate that was injurious to Kateřina's precari-

[1] 'Vzpomínky na Smetanu', in *Dalibor*, vol. vii, 1885, pp. 175–7; Bartoš, *op. cit.*, pp. 45–7.
[2] Thörnqvist, *op. cit.*

ous state of health, and declared that he intended to leave Göteborg for good. He would probably have to return to teaching in Prague, and on this point he had some significant things to say: 'My adorable situation, my rapture, my sweetest desire—I shall doubtless have to resume once more, but in no circumstances shall I start a school again.'[1] Three years later, in rather different circumstances, he broke this resolve. Having waited for the worst of the winter to pass, Smetana set off with Kateřina for home. But as they approached Dresden she became so seriously ill that they could go no farther. She died there on 19th April 1859.

While the composer was still reeling under this tragic blow, Liszt suggested that he should attend the silver jubilee celebrations in Leipzig of Schumann's paper, *Neue Zeitschrift für Musik*, and he agreed with alacrity. During those first four days of June he heard Bach's B minor Mass, Schumann's *Genoveva*, and for the second time Liszt's *Estergom Mass*. He also heard a striking extract from Wagner's newest and most advanced composition, the prelude to *Tristan and Isolde*, and this made a deep impression on him. After this he spent a few days as Liszt's guest at Weimar. He played his two symphonic poems to Liszt, and his Piano Trio was performed in the town. He met Hans von Bülow, the Russian critic Alexander Serov and other interesting people, and had absorbing discussions on the New Music with Liszt. After returning to Bohemia he became deeply attracted by his brother Karel's sister-in-law, Bettina Ferdinandová. She did not love him, but did admire him, and he had favourably impressed her parents; so Bedřich and Bettina became engaged. Since he was free to return to Göteborg he set off for another season there with a lighter heart. He stopped on the way in Copenhagen to meet Gade, just as he had done on his way home in May 1857.

Smetana was as busy as ever during the winter of 1859–60. He paid homage to Mozart by conducting his Requiem on the anniversary of

[1] Letter to Anna Kolářová, January 1859. The original German makes the irony clearer still: 'Die allerliebsten Konditionen, meine Wonne, mein süssester Wunsch—werden wohl wieder aufgenommen werden müssen, doch errichte ich auf keinen Fall eine Schule mehr.' Rychnovsky, *op. cit.*, p. 78.

his death, performed the second part of *Elijah* on 23rd January and presented *Messiah* on 25th April. The Harmoniska Sällskapet orchestra made heavy weather of Smetana's *Triumphal Symphony* at rehearsal, but were able to give it an acceptable performance on 31st March. In the same programme Smetana played Weber's *Concert-stück* in F minor, Liszt's first *Hungarian Rhapsody* and other pieces. Ole Bull, the Norwegian violinist, took part in the last chamber music soirée on 21st April, and on the 27th, at Ferdinand Laub's concert, Laub and Smetana played Beethoven's *Kreutzer* Sonata.

Instead of following *Wallenstein's Camp* with another Schiller symphonic poem based on *Wallenstein's Death* as he had planned, Smetana turned instead to the Danish poet Öhlenschläger's dramatic masterpiece, *Haakon Jarl*, for inspiration for his next big orchestral work. He began this early in 1860, but it was not finished until more than a year later. Among his less ambitious works were the *Memories of Bohemia* in polka form, Opp. 12 and 13, and *Betty's Polka*, a piece that Bettina asked him to write, but which disappointed her. He dedicated Op. 12 to Fröjda and Op. 13 to Bettina.

Meanwhile the defeat of Franz Josef's army by Napoleon III at Magenta and Solferino in June 1859 delighted the Czechs and was having interesting consequences. Alexander Bach was dismissed and a period of political experimentation began, a gradual thaw which resulted eight years later in the establishment of a constitutional monarchy for Greater Austria and Hungary. As soon as the Emperor found it necessary to give way to at least some of the mounting pressures, it became apparent that there was a brighter future in store for Czech culture. Smetana was glad that his patriotic friends remembered him in his exile, and was delighted when his former pupil Dr Ludevít Procházka asked him to write a male voice chorus for his collection *Záboj*. His patriotism was aroused, and so he replied with some difficulty in Czech, saying: 'I need hardly repeat that I am a Czech, heart and soul, and am proud to be an heir to our glory. Therefore I am not ashamed to reply to you in my mother tongue, however imperfectly, and am glad to be able to show that my fatherland means more to me than anything else.'[1] After returning to

[1] Letter of 11th March 1860; K. Teige, *Dopisy Smetanovy*, pp. 38–9.

Bohemia he set Jan z Hvězdy's poem the *Czech Song*. The signs were unmistakable. Smetana knew that he would soon be obliged to sever his ties with Sweden because his people needed him. Who else was there who could provide his country with worthy and truly national compositions?

Smetana remarried on 10th July 1860 and returned to Göteborg with Bettina six weeks later for one final season. He performed Haydn's *Creation* on 20th December and repeated it on 16th February. The chamber music soirées commenced after Christmas, and because Meissner had departed and been replaced by Grosse the programmes were more restricted in scope and enterprise. A farewell concert was given on 19th March, and then Smetana went to Stockholm where he played before the royal family at the Royal Theatre on 10th April. He was particularly successful when he returned to the theatre three days later to play Beethoven's C minor Concerto. He failed to make anything out of his chamber concert on the 23rd, but was recompensed by his appearance at Norrköping on 2nd May, where he made a profit of 150 riksdaler. The happy pair reached home on 19th May, and on the 25th September their daughter Zděnka was born.

Before settling down permanently in Prague Smetana decided to make himself better known by doing a tour of Germany and Holland. It proved impossible to arrange a concert at Leipzig, so he went on to Cologne, where he played the familiar Beethoven Concerto, his new concert study *on the Seashore* and Liszt's *Rigoletto* Fantasia at the Conservatory on 9th November. He met the ageing František Škroup when he reached Rotterdam. The Dutch part of his tour was again marred by inefficient organization, and when he played to students at Leiden on the 26th his reward was meagre. He played Beethoven's *Archduke* Trio at Cologne on 10th December, but his concert at Amsterdam planned for the 13th was cancelled, so he hurried home with very little to show for all his trouble.[1]

In the concert hall on Žofin (Sophia) Island, Prague, during a snowstorm on the night of 5th January 1862, Smetana conducted the

---

[1] Smetana's letters to his wife from Germany and Holland appear in Rychnovsky, *op. cit.*

first orchestral performance of *Richard III* and *Wallenstein's Camp* and played Beethoven's C minor Piano Concerto before a miserably small audience. In his diary he commented: 'A prophet is without honour in his own land.' As for the critics, the Czech newspapers showed tolerance, whereas the German press blamed him for adhering to the neo-German school and even out-Liszting Liszt.[1] They were quite unprepared for anything so advanced. Smetana's diary continues: 'If the neo-German school means progress, then I belong to it; at least I always take pains to write as I feel without taking notice of anything else.' When he gave a solo recital on 18th January the Konvict Hall was packed, which was encouraging, but the twenty-four gulden he made from the concert made no amends for the deficit of well over two hundred gulden on the previous venture.

When Nissen invited Smetana to revisit Göteborg, the composer leapt at the idea of returning to a city where he knew he was appreciated and where he had so many good friends. He therefore set off on 8th March on his last visit to Sweden. While he was in Göteborg he did some teaching and made three public appearances. At his first concert on 26th March he was the soloist in Mendelssohn's G minor Piano Concerto, he played several solos and was joined by Czapek in Beethoven's A minor Violin Sonata, Op. 23. At the concerts on 10th April and 2nd May he played a selection of solos, the Beethoven Violin Sonata in G, Op. 30, No. 3, and Beethoven's first Piano Trio. After two months he left and reached home by the middle of May, well satisfied because, financially as well as artistically, this short visit had been most rewarding.

[1]F. B. Ulm in *Bohemia*, 6th January 1862.

CHAPTER V

THE FLOWERING OF CZECH NATIONALISM

Smetana was delighted to hear that the new Provisional Theatre in Prague would be used for opera and operetta as well as for spoken drama, and this was undoubtedly the decisive factor that impelled him to leave Sweden. He was also greatly interested in Count Jan von Harrach's offer of two prizes of six hundred gulden each for the best historical and comic operas on Czech subjects. Up to that time Smetana had not been directly concerned with opera, but he recognized its great importance in national culture. Whereas symphonic music had a less universal and more limited appeal, opera was able to speak directly to the people. Without losing any time he approached the distinguished poet J. J. Kolár on 20th May 1861, the day after he arrived back from Sweden, hoping he would write a historical libretto for him. Kolár was so dilatory that Smetana was obliged to turn to Karel Sabina for help. Sabina responded promptly and in February 1862 the composer received from him the text for his first opera, *The Brandenburgers in Bohemia*.

Count Harrach associated closely with the group of traditionalist patriots known as the *staročeši* (Old Czech Party), and not with the radical group, the *mladočeši* (Young Czech Party). It was natural therefore that he should insist that the prize-winning operas be based on his country's folk-songs. This condition was strongly resented by Smetana, who had no wish to have his hands tied. During the period, when final preparations were being made for the Provisional Theatre, Dr F. L. Rieger, a leading *staročech* politician, stated in a discussion on Czech opera that it was a simple matter to write a historical opera, but much more difficult to compose a light opera dealing with the life of the people. When Rieger added that such an opera would have to be based on folk-songs, Smetana refuted this sharply. He retorted that 'in this way a medley of different songs would arise, a sort of

31

quodlibet, but not a unified artistic work'.[1] As an angry parting shot he asserted that Rieger was not qualified to give an opinion in this matter; and so he made this powerful and influential man into an enemy for life.

When the conductorship of the Provisional Theatre was being decided, Smetana was disappointed to find he was not being considered for the post. In the eyes of the *staročeši* he was too dangerous a modernist. Instead the appointment went to J. N. Maýr, whose experience of singing and conducting was much greater than Smetana's; as a musician, however, he was uninspiring. Amid great rejoicing the theatre was opened on 18th November 1862 with a performance of V. Hálek's play *King Vakušín*. The first opera was presented two days later, but as no sufficiently worthy Czech opera existed to mark such an occasion, and it would have been inappropriate to have selected a German or Austrian work, Cherubini's 'rescue' opera *The Water Carrier* was chosen.

Once again it became necessary for Smetana to resume teaching, and in partnership with the violinist and conductor Ferdinand Heller he opened another music school, which proved to be no more remunerative than the previous one. He again paid regular visits to the Emperor Ferdinand, and also became a music critic. In articles written for *Slavoj* (1862) and *Národní listy* (1864) he emphasized the need for a forward-looking policy for opera and symphony concerts, but he had little chance of putting his ideas into practice. He gave the first performance of *Haakon Jarl* at an Academic Readers' Society concert on 24th February 1864. The tercentenary of Shakespeare's birth was celebrated by a concert on 23rd April sponsored by the Umělecká beseda (Artistic Circle). Smetana was in his element, for he conducted Berlioz's *Romeo and Juliet* and his own newly composed *March for the Shakespearean Festival*. He must have been pleased too when he became conductor of the Prague Hlahol Choral Society in 1863. But when he tried launching a series of three subscription concerts during the 1864–5 season, introducing music by his compatriots J. J. Abert, J. B. Kittl and J. L. Zvonař, and performing extracts from his

---

[1] Related by J. Srb-Debrnov; Bartoš, *op. cit.*

Brandenburgers, together with Glinka's *Kamarinskaya* and a selection of classical and contemporary works, he ran into trouble. His venture was poorly supported and he again lost money. Kittl's resignation from the directorship of the Prague Conservatory in 1865 raised Smetana's hopes that he might secure this important and influential position. František Pivoda, the founder of the Prague School of Singing, gave him his full support, but Smetana also found it was essential to curry favour with the aristocracy, with whom he had lost touch. His strongest claim to the post was that his achievement as a composer was outstanding, but unfortunately this was not generally recognized. Josef Krejčí became the new director.

During this period Smetana made rapid strides in composition. By 23rd April 1863 he had completed *The Brandenburgers in Bohemia*. Two months earlier, on 19th February, Bettina's second daughter, Božena, had been born. Smetana wrote several smaller compositions, including the male-voice choruses, *The Three Riders* and *The Renegade*, and overtures to the puppet plays, *Faust* and *Oldřich and Božena*. But he was very anxious to compose a second opera, and when Sabina provided him with another libretto on 5th July 1863 he was able to commence the stage work that directly challenged Rieger's arguments: *The Bartered Bride*. The new work was finished on 15th March 1866, but eleven months earlier he had already begun to make sketches for his third opera, *Dalibor*.

In the spring of 1865, following some months of inaction, rehearsals of *The Brandenburgers in Bohemia* were started, but since Maýr disliked Smetana and took little interest in his work progress was unsatisfactory. Towards the end of the year Maýr decided to wash his hands of this opera, thus leaving the way clear for Smetana to prepare and conduct it. For the composer this was a heaven-sent opportunity. When it was first performed on 5th January 1866 the opera was a great success, and it was then given ten more performances to enthusiastic audiences. No work of such calibre had ever been written previously by a Czech composer. This success had three important consequences: somewhat reluctantly, the jury agreed that Smetana deserved the Harrach prize; the theatre management consented to perform *The Bartered Bride*, and this was first presented on 30th May; and, best of all, Smetana's triumph was directly responsible for his appointment as principal conductor of the theatre at an annual salary of 1,200 gulden, a post he held for eight years. Curious as it may at first seem, when *The Bartered Bride* was first performed, in its simpler version with spoken dialogue, it was a failure, but this was entirely due to the unsettled political atmosphere on the eve of the Austro-Prussian war. Fearing that he might be in some danger because he had composed *The Brandenburgers in Bohemia*, Smetana thought it prudent to vanish from Prague before the Prussians arrived, and so for a month he and his family stayed near Beroun at the parental home of one of his music school teachers.

Maýr worked hard while he was the sole conductor of the Provisional Theatre. He built up a repertory of between fifty and sixty operas, gave over three hundred and fifty performances in three and a half years and conducted practically every opera himself. At that time the only Czech operas to draw upon were Škroup's *The Tinker*, Skuherský's *Vladimír, God's Chosen One*, Šebor's *The Templars in Moravia* and Smetana's first two works, so most of the operas performed were Italian, French or German. Although approximately seventeen Italian and seventeen French operas were given, the number of performances of Italian works exceeded the French works by two to one, and reached a total of almost 150. Smetana disliked Maýr's pronounced Italian bias; he was determined to redress the balance during his period of office, and succeeded in doing so.[1] For the opening night of his first opera season (26th September 1866) he chose to conduct *Der Freischütz*.

Balakirev had previously persuaded Maýr to mount *A Life for the Czar*, and he now continued his efforts to arrange for performances of Glinka's works. He was extremely shocked by Smetana's treatment

---

[1] According to information I have received from Jarmil Burghauser, during the first fifteen months of Smetana's conductorship eleven Italian operas were given forty-eight performances, seven French operas were performed forty times, seven German operas were performed twenty-five times, seven Czech operas were performed thirty-seven or thirty-eight times, and two Russian operas were performed thirteen times. Smetana conducted ninety-six performances, and his assistant Adolf Čech directed nearly fifty, in addition to all the incidental music in plays.

of this same work, which he saw early in January 1867. In his customary interfering way he must have shown Smetana how annoyed
he was, and consequently aroused the Czech composer's wrath. This
would certainly explain why the two men were at loggerheads, and also
suggests why the full score of *Ruslan and Lyudmila* mysteriously vanished
before the first performance on 16th February, thus forcing Balakirev
to conduct the entire work from memory. During the 1868 season
Halka by the Polish composer Moniuszko was performed, and when a
repeat performance was given on 1st May the composer was present.
There was a notable increase in the number of Czech operas that
became available during Smetana's conductorship, and during his
first six years the following works were performed for the first time:
J. N. Škroup's *The Swedes in Prague*; Šebor's *Drahomíra, Hussite
Bride* and *Blanka*; Blodek's *In the Well*; K. Bendl's *Lejla*; Vojáček's
Captured Maid; Bendl's *Břetislav*; Rozkošný's *Mikuláš* and *St John's
Rapids*; Měchura's *Marie Potocká*; and Smetana's *Dalibor*. In addition
to these Skuherský's *Lora*, which had been given previously in German
at Innsbruck, was presented in a Czech translation.

Josef Wenzig, the president of the Umělecká beseda, had provided
Smetana with a German libretto of *Dalibor*, which Ervín Špindler
then translated into Czech. As we see from a letter Smetana wrote to
his Swedish friend J. P. Valentin, the composer realized that a German
text opened up the possibility of performances abroad, and hoped
that these might materialize.[1] He composed the opera between 15th
April 1865 and 29th December 1867, and it was performed on a
very important occasion. The *mladočeši* was exceptionally active in
furthering the plan to build a permanent National Theatre, and the
foundation stone was laid on 16th May 1868 amid tremendous
national rejoicing. Karel Sladkovský delivered the oration, František
Palacký asked for the blessing of the Almighty, and Smetana, representing the Czech musicians, helped to drive the stone into the
ground, proclaiming: 'Music—the life of the Czechs!' In the evening
at the New Town Theatre Smetana's new *Festive Overture* was played,
J. J. Kolár's poem *The Prophesy of Libuše* was read, and *Dalibor* was
presented.

[1] Letter of 20th April 1865; Bartoš, *op. cit.*

When Smetana wrote this opera he was firmly convinced he was following the right path for Czech music. As a progressive composer he was keenly interested in the newer trends in contemporary music, and prepared to borrow ideas from them if it suited his purpose. His audience had no clear understanding of his aims, and the critics who thought that Czech opera should have a folk-song basis fancied that *Dalibor* was an example of full-blooded Wagnerism. The bad press notices had such a serious effect upon attendance at the repeat performances that the opera was dropped from the repertory after only five complete presentations. It reappeared in December 1870 but was given only six times, and subsequently three more times in 1879. This persistent rejection of a work for which Smetana had the highest regard was a bitter experience. It also marked the beginning of an unpleasant campaign of vilification and abuse.

CHAPTER VI

HOSTILITY AND DEAFNESS

During the years when Smetana was particularly active as a conductor there was much dissatisfaction over the status of Czechs in the empire. After the defeat of the Austrians by the Prussians at Sadowa, Franz Josef was persuaded to come to terms with the proud Hungarians. Early in 1867 he bowed to their wish to manage their own affairs, but retained control himself of imperial finance, foreign affairs and war. The remaining minorities became an indeterminate agglomeration of Czechs, Slovaks, Croats and Serbs, who had no responsible place in the newly formed Austro-Hungarian empire, and could not expect Hungarian aristocrats and German-speaking nobles and burgesses to be sympathetic. Smetana complained bitterly of the arrest of those who criticized the government and of the state of emergency of February and March 1869. In the autumn he was greatly heartened by the election results, and once more Franz Josef's coronation seemed likely. The Prime Minister, Count von Hohenwart, and the liberal Albert Schäffle planned to grant the Czechs autonomy, but there was dissension between Austrians and Czechs over the territorial division. Count Julius Andrássy, the Hungarian Prime Minister, knew that Austrian acceptance of national equality for the Czechs would undermine Hungary's privileged position, and took prompt action which led to Hohenwart's dismissal and his own promotion as the Emperor's Foreign Minister. There was no coronation, and the Czechs remained second-class citizens.

In the spring of 1866, long before he finished composing *Dalibor*, Smetana received Wenzig's German libretto for his most ambitious opera, *Libuše*, which was then translated into Czech by Špindler. Work on this probably began in the summer of 1869, but the full score was not finished until 12th November 1872. This was never intended to be a repertory opera, but one reserved for a great festive occasion like Franz Josef's coronation. More than eight years elapsed before the opening of the new National Theatre provided the right moment for it to be performed. While Smetana was at work on this epic and prophetic opera, Nápravník, the Czech-born conductor of the Russian Imperial Opera, gave a performance of *The Bartered Bride* before the Crown Prince, Grand Dukes and a crowded theatre at St Petersburg on 11th January 1871. The enthusiastic audience applauded every number. Several days later Smetana was distressed to discover how little interest the critics showed in his opera, and he felt insulted that Famintsin should have said that it was no better than Offenbach. Meanwhile one of the critics at home was already proving to be an even greater thorn in his flesh.

When Smetana became chief conductor of the Provisional Theatre, Pivoda took it for granted that his school of singing would be the training ground for the soloists. Once he discovered that Smetana was travelling to Olomouc, Brno and Vienna to find new talent he was greatly offended, and could not bring himself to forgive his friend. He had written very favourable criticisms of Smetana's music earlier on, but when *Dalibor* was performed he maintained a strict silence, so that it would not be seen that he had made a *volte face*. Writing in *Pokrok*,[1] Pivoda complained that Bendl's *Lejla* had not been heard for a long time, and added that the prospects for Czech opera were not bright because 'apart from Mr Smetana, who does not stand in his own way . . . our leading composers are pushed aside. . . .' Smetana replied in *Národní listy*,[2] explaining that there were substantial technical reasons why the revivals of *Lejla* was delayed. *The Brandenburgers* was revived after almost two years for his benefit night, but *Dalibor* had been dropped. *The Bartered Bride* was useful as a stop-gap, but it was absurd to claim that performances of this work gave him a monopoly over other composers. Besides, what right had Pivoda to moan about the prospects for Czech opera when he based the work of his school of singing on Verdi and did not prepare his pupils for Czech opera?

[1] 22nd February 1870.
[2] 26th February 1870.

SMETANA AND HIS WIFE BETTINA IN 1860

In his next attack [1] Pivoda accused Smetana of being an extreme Wagnerian, of implying it was hopeless to attempt to foster Czech opera, and of being pathologically jealous of Šebor's *Drahomíra* (which Šebor himself conducted on 20th September 1867). He admitted that he had genuinely believed that Smetana was the man best fitted to establish Czech opera, and in doing so had overlooked his faults. He now blamed himself for his error of judgment. He also declared he had recognized Smetana as an enemy from the first. It was becoming clear that Pivoda was a slippery customer. Smetana, on the other hand, was at a disadvantage when using the Czech language, and was liable to misinterpret Pivoda's innuendos and to say more than was prudent when he was roused. He was infuriated by Pivoda's long letter, and in his reply [2] said that the critic did not know what Wagnerism was, and challenged him to prove there was as much national character in all the operas of his so-called rivals as in one-third of *Dalibor*. Pivoda side-stepped this issue and piously asserted [3] that he could not join Smetana in mud-slinging and self-praise, which were unworthy of an educated man. In addition he asked for proof that he had ever raved furiously at Smetana.

When Smetana met Otakar Hostinský at Munich soon after the first performance of *Dalibor*, the latter suggested to him that Czech music would follow Wagner's lead sooner or later, to which Smetana replied: 'Of course, but not now; it is absolutely impossible at present. Progress like that must be prepared gradually, and at the same time we must proceed in our own way in accordance with our own special circumstances.' [4] Smetana made the most of his opportunities to become familiar with Wagner's music, and when he was in Munich again in July 1870 he saw *Das Rheingold* and went to *Die Walküre* three times.

Smetana was not drawn into further controversy for some time, but during 1872 Pivoda aired his views on the future path of Czech opera

[1] *Pokrok*, 3rd March 1870.

[2] *Národní listy*, 8th March 1870.

[3] *Pokrok*, 10th March 1870.

[4] O. Hostinský, *Bedřich Smetana a jeho bo jo moderní českou hudbu* (Prague, 1901), p. 132; Bartoš, *op. cit.*

in *Osvĕta*.[1] His unrealistic plan for an equal interchange of Czech opera with opera in other countries need not detain us here. More important is his assertion that Czech composers should avoid complexity and aim for a noble simplicity in all their stage works, a shaft that was directed straight at Smetana. Hostinský replied to Pivoda in a series of carefully reasoned articles that he wrote for *Hudební listy*,[2] during the course of which he declared that true national art must be as all-embracing as possible and therefore cannot stem solely from folk art. Neither need its subject be limited to the history or everyday life of the nation. It must arise naturally and the pace of progress must not be forced. It should utilize all foreign elements that are beneficial to it, even the most modern. Later, when these have been assimilated, the art's fundamental core, its basic national spirit and character, will have a chance to emerge and predominate.

It was extremely irritating for Smetana that during the whole of his conductorship the theatre's intendant should have been the hostile *staročech* Dr F. L. Rieger, but at least he had a strong supporter in the vice-chairman, Dr Antonín Čízek. Rieger and his supporters hoped to oust Smetana from his post and reappoint Maýr. To counteract the mounting pressure, Dvořák, Skuherský, Bendl, Fibich, Roskošný, Hřímalý and other prominent musicians drafted a strongly worded memorandum, virtually an ultimatum, on 17th October 1872, supporting Smetana loyally. But since the co-ordinating committee was already discussing terms for his reappointment this document was not sent. Early in December eighty-six subscribers called for Smetana's dismissal, but a month later his reappointment was confirmed; his salary was raised to 2,000 gulden and he was given increased responsibilities.[3]

The public was becoming restive because no new opera by Smetana had been produced since *Dalibor*. It was not easy for him to turn his attention to a new work when he was being harassed by enemies, but he found it possible to start on his fifth opera, *The Two Widows*, on 16th July 1873, and he made such rapid progress that the score was

[1] pp. 235–40 and 548–53.
[2] Vol. iii (1872), nos. 32–8 inclusive.
[3] Hostinský, *op. cit.*, pp. 272–6.

completed by 15th January 1874. For this work Emanuel Züngl had adapted Félicien Mallefille's comedy *Les deux veuves*, transferring the setting to Bohemia. The opera was very warmly received on 27th March, but some press notices were unfavourable.

When Pivoda resumed his attack on Smetana in an unsigned article in *Hudební listy* early in 1874 [1] his main purpose was to discredit Smetana's artistic administration. He claimed that the theatre had thrived with Maýr as conductor, but that the position in 1874 was the exact reverse of this. Whereas Maýr had built up the organization in an incredibly short time and, unaided, had prepared fifty-seven operas in barely four years, Smetana, he said, had prepared only eleven of the forty-two operas newly performed during his seven years as conductor. V. Linhardt followed this up with an article in *Politik* [2] listing the operas referred to by Pivoda. The unfairness of this comparison is manifest, because it was Smetana's duty to consolidate and improve the repertory established by Maýr, rather than to enlarge it greatly. Besides this, Smetana shared his duties with his assistant, whereas Maýr was in sole command. Smetana was greatly upset by this fresh show of hostility, and in his first reply [3] pointed out that during his 'most unhappy year', 1873, almost as many operas were performed in only nine months as during the whole of Maýr's 'most brilliant season', 1863–4. In claiming that he was personally responsible for thirty-three of the eighty-two new productions mounted during his conductorship, Smetana unwisely added that he had to prepare all the operas afresh 'if for no other reason than that I was unable to agree with the way they were performed previously'. This gave Maýr an opportunity to say: [4] 'Quite apart from the fact that he made himself judge in his own cause, I cannot understand how Mr Smetana can sport such boundless arrogance in public.' Whilst Pivoda slyly remarked that Smetana may have needed 'to prepare the operas in order to get to know them better'. [5]

[1] 22nd and 29th January and 5th February.
[2] 18th February 1874.
[3] *Politik*, 25th February 1874.
[4] *Politik*, 8th March 1874.
[5] *Hudební listy*, 5th March 1874.

When Smetana answered Pivoda in *Hudební listy* [1] he found himself being subjected to further insinuations and accusations of scandal, the most serious of which was the charge that under his leadership 'Czech opera sickens to death at least once annually'. Since he could not expect fair treatment from Skrejšovský's *staročech* paper, he then replied in *Dalibor*,[2] a paper which had just been relaunched by his friends Hostinský and Procházka. Maýr, he said, had caused much amusement when he chose absurd tempi in Beethoven's Eighth Symphony, and displayed his ignorance of the rules of harmony when making cuts in *The Jewess*, so he had no right to criticize others.[3]

Smetana recorded in his diary on 30th April that he had had a purulent ulcer since the 12th, without indicating where it was located. He complained on 11th June that his throat had been troubling him for about a fortnight, and on the 28th he stated that there was no sign of the trouble clearing up. When a rash appeared on his body in mid July he travelled to Prague to see his doctor, but was assured that it was not serious.[4] Then on 28th July he wrote: 'My ears are blocked and at the same time my head seems to swim and I feel giddy. It started after a little duck-shooting, and just before that the weather had changed suddenly.' Early in August Professor E. Zoufal, the otologist, had him under observation; he told him that the blockage was due to catarrh, and prescribed deep breathing. Smetana was unable to continue with his work, and so *Dalibor* published the following statement on 15th August: 'The conductor, Bedřich Smetana, has become ill as the result of nervous strain caused by certain people recently. His nerves are in so serious a state that he must give up all music and avoid all mental exertion for a while, and in general must take the greatest care of himself.' His ear trouble was not mentioned, but the paper added that Karel Bendl would assist Čech at the theatre.

Professor Zoufal tried to relieve Smetana's trouble on 3rd September

---

[1] 26th February 1874.

[2] 21st March 1874.

[3] For a much fuller account of the whole subject, see my article: 'The Smetana-Pivoda Controversy', *Music and Letters*, vol. 52, no. 4 (1971).

[4] Diary entry, 14th July 1874.

with an air spray, and then on the 15th with a catheter. His condition, however, was so serious that he was obliged to write to his vice-chairman, Dr Čizek, on 7th September as follows:[1]

I feel it to be my duty to tell you of the cruel fate that has overtaken me. I may lose my hearing. I can hear nothing at all with my right ear and only indifferently with my left. This is my present state even though I have been having treatment since July. During July, on the second day after the dress rehearsal, I noticed that I heard the notes in the higher octaves with each ear at different pitches, and that I sometimes had a buzzing and tingling in my ears as if I were standing by a huge waterfall. My condition changed frequently until the end of July, when it became a permanent state and when I had attacks of giddiness, which made me stagger to and fro, so that I could only walk straight by concentrating hard. I had a wretched holiday.

I hurried from the country to Prague to be treated by Dr Zoufal, the eminent doctor in this field. He is still treating me. He has forbidden me all effort and all musical activity. I can neither play nor listen to others playing, and a large choir becomes a jumble of sound, so that I am unable to distinguish the individual parts.

I beg you therefore to inform the committee of the Association about my unfortunate condition—which is really disastrous—and since I cannot carry out my duties, please request them to release me from my work of conducting and rehearsing for an indefinite period. If during the next three months my health deteriorates, then I shall be obliged to resign my post at the theatre and surrender myself to my fate.[2]

He ended his letter with a request for fees due to him for his teaching work at the operatic school, which he needed badly because he was losing his main source of income.

On 8th October, four days after Zoufal had used an ether douche, Smetana wrote in his diary: 'For the first time for ages I can again hear

[1] Bartoš, *op. cit.*

[2] The most comprehensive study of Smetana's medical case history is H. Feldmann's article, 'Die Krankheit Friedrich Smetanas in otologischer Sicht', in *Monatsschrift für Ohrenheilkunde u. Laryngo-Rhinologie*, vol. 98, no. 5 (Vienna, 1964), pp. 209–26. English translation in *Music Review*, vol. 32.

the entire range of octaves in tune. Hithero they were jumbled up. I can still hear nothing with my right ear.' But this improvement did not last. On 20th October he became deaf in his left ear. In a very depressed state he wrote in his diary on the 30th: 'For almost a week I have had to stay at home; I can't go out, my ears are wrapped in cotton wool and I must keep absolutely quiet. I fear the worst, that I have become completely deaf, for I hear nothing. How long will this continue? Shall I ever recover?—!!!' And on 30th November he wrote: 'My ear trouble is just as it was at the beginning of this month. I cannot hear anything either with my right or my left ear. Dr Zoufal hasn't given up hope but I have. If only that continual noise would stop!'

Smetana told J. Srb-Debrnov that he heard some exquisite flute playing when walking in the woods in August that year, and heard it again next day at home, but in neither case was there a flautist to be seen.[1] When he wrote to Bettina from Copenhagen on 11th March 1862 he mentioned another aural illusion, but there does not appear to be any connection between the two events.[2]

Despite the tragic turn of events *Politik* revived its feud against Smetana in the early autumn. He was accused of accepting an annual salary of six hundred gulden from the opera school for only two hours' teaching a week. When he ignored this statement this was taken to mean that the allegation was true, which provoked him to reply. He pointed out in *Hudební listy* [3] that he was paid solely to direct the school, yet he also taught theory, examined all the pianists and conducted the orchestra as well. During this time he found some consolation in composing. *Vyšehrad*. the first of the cycle of six symphonic poems, *My Fatherland*, was begun towards the end of September and finished on 18th November, and *Vltava* was written between 20th November and 8th December. He was engaged on the third work *Šárka* from January until 20th February 1875.

He was not satisfied when he heard the Theatre Association proposed to give him only 1,200 gulden annually for the right to perform

[1] 'Návštěva v Jabkenících', in *Dalibor*, vol. iii, 1881.

[2] Rychnovsky, *op. cit.*, pp. 139–40.

[3] 29th September 1874.

his operas, and complained bitterly to Bubeniček, the chairman, asking for more, so that he would not slowly starve and would have an incentive to continue composing. Bubeniček pointed out that there was a serious financial deficit, and advised him to accept in case the next offer was less favourable.[1] Smetana's former pupil, Countess Elisabeth Kaunitz, *née* Thun, arranged for his pupils to give a concert on 23rd February at her home in order to collect funds for him. *Politik* raised its voice in protest against this friendly gesture. It was unnecessary, it said, because Smetana had been nobly and generously treated by the Association. Jan Neruda immediately replied, giving strong support to his friend in *Národní listy*.[2] Smetana informed Charlotte Valentin, a Swedish friend, about his deafness, and later asked Fröjda Benecke if she could arrange a concert in Göteborg to ease his financial straits. Early in April he received from these two and several other of his friends there a draft for 1,244 gulden,[3] which enabled him to seek the advice of specialists outside Bohemia.

On Dr Zoufal's recommendation Smetana travelled to Würzburg to have daily consultations between 20th and 25th April with Dr Tröltsch, and next he got in touch with the Viennese specialist Politzer. In his letter to him he mentioned that Zoufal had begun to inflate the middle ear on both sides at the end of February. He also stated that there had been a slight improvement since March which had enabled him to hear high-pitched vowels and sibilants, although these were distorted and sounded like the crackling of small sticks.[4] He visited Politzer on 5th May, and was told by him that he suffered from paralysis of the inner ear, and that he must have electrical therapy and use an ear trumpet. Later that month Zoufal ordered him to have complete silence and isolation for a month, without communicating with anyone, even in writing, and he was given an ointment to use behind his ears and all over his body. When Zoufal tested his hearing on 20th June he declared he was satisfied, but Smetana was unable to notice any improvement. The composer pinned his greatest faith on

---

[1] Smetana's letter of 6th January and the reply appear in Bartoš, *op. cit.*
[2] 27th and 28th February 1875.
[3] Rychnovsky, *op. cit.*, pp. 232–4.
[4] Draft of letter written at the beginning of May; Feldmann, *op. cit.*

the electrical therapy. He told Bendl that he was going to have a course of treatment from Hagen at Leipzig in the autumn, and commented: 'The last attempt. Then my fate will be sealed.' [1] However, there was no need to make this journey because Zoufal installed similar electrical equipment at that time. But the treatment was a failure. On his fifty-second birthday Smetana wrote these words in his diary: 'If my illness is incurable, then I should prefer to be delivered from this miserable existence.'

[1] Letter of 24th July 1875; Bartoš, *op. cit.*

CHAPTER VII

THE FINAL PHASE

In spite of the bleak outlook for the future there were encouraging signs that a large section of the public was loyal to Smetana and that their admiration for him as a composer was growing. When Ludvík Slánský gave the first performance of *Vyšehrad* on 14th March 1875 the audience insisted on the work being played twice. Smetana was delighted to witness the warm reception, but was not able to hear a single note. *Vltava* was also a success when Adolf Čech conducted it on 4th April. Smetana completed a fourth symphonic poem, *From Bohemia's Fields and Forests*, on 18th October. When Čech performed this on 10th December 1876, this also had to be repeated. He gave the first performance of *Šárka* on 17th March 1877.

Eliška Krásnohorská had given Smetana in 1871 an opera libretto based on *Twelfth Night* and called *Viola*, and three years later he began making sketches for this, without much progress. When he asked her in 1875 for another libretto she suggested using Karolina Světlá's *The Kiss*, but he was not at all convinced that this would be suitable until she handed him verses for the courting scene. He immediately saw that they were made for music. She sent him the libretto on 11th November, and except for the overture the whole opera was finished by 29th July 1876. When the new work was performed on 7th November it proved to be another triumph. Miss Krásnohorská found it embarrassing that the deaf composer always shouted when he spoke, without being conscious that he was doing so. When they met in the street one day he bellowed out that he was so pleased she had given him that *Kiss*.[1]

The Theatre Association was very dilatory over paying Smetana his agreed salary, and he blamed Maýr for this. He was forced to give

[1] E. Krásnohorská, *Vzpominky půlstoleté*; Bartoš, *op. cit.*

47

notice to his Prague landlord in April 1876, and on 3rd June he settled permanently with his daughter Žofie and son-in-law Josef Schwarz at Jabkenice, near Mladá Boleslav, where they lived in Count Hugo von Taxis's gamekeeper's lodge. Smetana's March salary did not arrive until the end of July. Towards the end of that year he wrote his first string quartet, *From My Life*, finishing it on 29th December. He explained why he gave the violin a high sustained harmonic at the end in a letter to Liszt's violinist friend August Kömpel:[1] 'I felt I must describe the onset of my deafness, and tried to represent this with the e^{iv} of the first violin in the finale of my quartet. Before I became completely deaf I was haunted every evening between six and seven by the shrill whistle of a first inversion chord of A flat in the highest register of the piccolo. This went on without interruption for half an hour and often for a whole hour, and I was unable to get rid of it.'

When Josef Srb-Debrnov asked Smetana to set Hálek's *Song of the Sea* for the Hlahol Choral Society, he would not commit himself while he was busy with his quartet, and also because, as he said,[2] 'my illness does not allow me to compose continuously for more than an hour. After that I have to stop work because a buzzing sound in my ears usually begins and makes it impossible for me to continue.' However, by 26th January the part-song was written, and the four polkas that form the first part of the *Czech Dances* for piano followed in April.

It was probably when Smetana visited Miss Krásnohorská on 10th December that he became enthusiastic about one of the subjects she suggested for his next opera. One of the attractions was that the scenic setting proposed for *The Secret* was the town of Bělá and the ruins of Bezděz castle, because of the historic abduction of the Bohemian Crown Prince to Bezděz in 1279, an event recorded in Smetana's *Brandenburgers*. While sketching the new opera he ran into serious trouble from the *staročeši*. Owing to the reorganization of the Theatre Association, his salary was withheld for several months

[1] Letter of 23rd May 1880.
[2] Letter to Srb-Debrnov, 20th December 1876; V. Balthasar, *Bedřich Smetana* (Prague, 1924), p. 125.

until it could be approved by the new committee. He ran completely out of money, and on 26th September 1877 he wrote to Dr Procházka asking him to petition the Association on his behalf.[1] In a letter to his librettist written on 2nd October he revealed his state of mind when he said:[2]

'I am afraid my music is not cheerful enough [for a comedy]. But how could I be cheerful? Where could happiness come from when my heart is heavy with trouble and sorrow? I should like ... to be able to work without having to worry. But unfortunately those gentlemen of the Association—and Fate—will not allow that. ... When I continually see only poverty and misery ahead of me all enthusiasm for my work goes, or at least my cheerful mood vanishes. Nevertheless please send me the second act soon. When I plunge into a musical ecstasy, then for a while I forget everything that persecutes me so cruelly in my old age.'

He wrote again to Procházka on 10th October, and later that month the Association paid him for the first time since May. When his contract was renewed he was most upset because he was forced to concede that *The Kiss* be added to the four operas on which he received no royalties. He therefore lost the revenue from his second most popular opera.

Although he was unable to work continuously, Smetana finished *The Secret*, including the overture, by 15th July 1878. Next day he sent a bitter letter to Dr Robert Nittinger,[3] the secretary of the Association, for he had heard that they were only going to allow him to have one benefit with this work. The opera was warmly received on 18th September when Čech conducted it at the New Town Theatre, and Felix Mottl was impressed by it. He hoped to mount *The Bartered Bride* in Vienna, but the fire at the Ringtheater prevented this. Two months after completing *The Secret* Smetana revised his *Czech Song* and scored it for orchestra, and during the winter he was occupied with two more symphonic poems, *Tábor* and *Blaník*, which complete

[1] J. Löwenbach, *B. Smetana a Dr L. Procházka* (Prague, 1914), pp. 21–4.
[2] M. Očadlík, *Eliška Krásnohorská—Bedřich Smetana* (Prague, 1940), pp. 85–7. He was already seriously estranged from his wife Bettina; see B. Large, *Smetana* (London, 1970).
[3] Bartoš, *op. cit.*

his cycle *My Fatherland*. They were both performed at his jubilee concert on 4th January 1880.[1]

Smetana welcomed any opportunities to visit Prague, because this was the best antidote for his lonely existence in the country. He would watch the crowds in the streets, read newspapers in coffee houses and go to plays and operas. He was able to follow performances of any music he knew well by watching the conductor's baton, and on 29th March 1879 he watched the first performance of his quartet *From My Life* through opera glasses while half concealed at the side of the platform.[2] At Jabkenice he was introduced to several unfamiliar Czech dances by Suchý, a retired teacher who played the fiddle, and this probably stimulated him to add ten more dances to the *Czech Dances* for piano during the spring and summer of 1879. The concert commemorating the fiftieth anniversary of his first public appearance at the age of six took place on 4th January. Besides the two symphonic poems, the first performances of a new song cycle, *Evening Songs*, and *Czech Song* took place, and the deaf composer played Chopin's Nocturne in B major, his own Polka in A minor, and performed his Piano Trio. The audience was horrified to hear him shout out 'Pianissimo!' to the other two players during the trio. Nevertheless it was a most successful concert, and for Smetana a very moving occasion.

Miss Krásnohorská related that Smetana had no difficulty in imagining the sound of the instruments and voices when he read scores by other composers, but if he persisted too long he heard unpleasant noises. She quoted him as saying: [3]

> That ringing in my head, that noise . . . that is worst of all! Deafness would be a relatively tolerable condition if only all was quiet in my head. However, almost continuous internal noise which sometimes increases to a thunderous crashing tortures me greatly. This inexplicable pandemonium is pierced by the shrieking of voices, from strident whistles to ghastly bawling, as though furies and demons were bearing down on me in a violent rage. . . . I begin to wonder what the end will be. . . .

---

[1] F. A. Urbánek published all six symphonic poems for piano duet and the first, second and fourth in full score during 1879–81.

[2] E. Veil, *Vzpominky na Bedřicha Smetanu* (1917); Bartoš, *op. cit.*

[3] Krásnohorská, *Ze vzpomínek na B. Smetanu* (1923); Bartoš, *op. cit.*

When he wrote to his friend J. V. Karel, he said:[1]

> Believe me that I need all my courage and strength to keep myself from be-
> coming so desperate as to plan to use violence to end my suffering. Only
> the sight of my family and the thought that I must go on working for my
> people and my country keeps me alive and inspires me to new creation.

Smetana was tired of composing crowd scenes, trials and big
ensembles, and wanted his next opera to be quite different, with
if possible a comic character like Rossini's Dr Bartolo or the mayor
in *Czar and Carpenter*.[2] With Miss Krásnohorská's help he decided
on the legend of Petr Vok, Lord of Rožmberk, with a thirteenth-
century setting and the title *The Devil's Wall*. He received the third
act of her libretto on 9th September 1879, but owing to the deterioration of his health his progress was extremely slow and the whole work,
without the overture, was not finished until 17th April 1882.

In the spring of 1881 preparations were made for the long-awaited
performance of *Libuše* at the official opening of the permanent National
Theatre, the date of which was advanced to 11th June so that the
Crown Prince could be present. Smetana attended the rehearsals
and was delighted with the enthusiasm of the singers, but he was disappointed to find the management was economizing over the production. When the great day came Smetana had not been given any
tickets for the performance. He wandered around the theatre until,
rather grudgingly, he was invited into the director's box. He was presented to the Crown Prince, but this was embarrassing because the
imperial guest was entirely unaware that the composer was stone deaf.
The audience was restrained while the prince was there, but when he
left they let themselves go, and called Smetana back many times. The
Theatre Association planned to pass over *Libuše* on the opening night
of the autumn season in favour of *Dimitrij* by Dvořák, who had already
won an international reputation. Smetana was particularly offended by
this, because Marie Červinková, the daughter of his enemy Rieger,

---

[1] Letter of 17th January 1880; M. Malý, *Jabkenická léta Bedřicha Smetany*
(1968), facsimile; Bartoš, *op. cit.*
[2] Letter to Krásnohorská, 31st January 1878; Očadlík, *op. cit.*

had written the libretto.[1] It would, however, have been impossible to perform *Dimitrij* because it was not completed until a year later. There was in fact no autumn season, for the whole nation was shocked to learn that their fine new theatre was completely destroyed by fire on 12th August.

After lengthy negotiations between Procházka and Bernard Pollini a contract was signed on 26th January 1881 for *The Two Widows* to be performed at Hamburg. It was so successful when it was presented on 28th December that the Berlin publishers Bote und Bock arranged to publish the vocal score within four weeks. Smetana was horrified when he heard this, for he knew that Roderich Fels's German translation changed the setting back from Bohemia to France and turned his refined salon comedy into something resembling Auber, Lecocq or Offenbach. His own artistic integrity was at stake. No wonder he remarked sadly: 'I have lost the wish to see my operas performed abroad.'[2] He made some revisions in August and September and added a trio, but made no concessions to public taste.

The hundredth performance of *The Bartered Bride* took place on 5th May 1882, and was celebrated with wreaths, presentations and a banquet. Even Maýr appears to have been affected by the importance of the occasion, for he immediately arranged a second 'hundredth performance' for all those who were unable to gain admission to the theatre. Smetana was acutely aware that all this fuss underlined one undeniable fact, that the audiences who flocked to see *The Bartered Bride* still failed to appreciate *Dalibor*, which he knew had far greater value. In his speech at the banquet he referred to his most successful work as 'only a trifle' which was written 'not out of vanity but for spite, because I was accused after *The Brandenburgers* of being a Wagnerian who was incapable of writing anything in a lighter vein'. [3]

When *The Devil's Wall* received its first performance on 29th October 1882 Smetana complained of 'bad décor, old costumes and

[1] Dvořák was prudent enough to ask the advice of Smetana's friend and supporter V. V. Zelený before starting to compose *Dimitrij*.

[2] The correspondence, the contract and press criticisms appear in J. Löwenbach, *op. cit.*

[3] *Dalibor*, vol. iv; Bartoš, *op. cit.*

too few rehearsals'. The third performance was a fiasco. This was his benefit night, yet no one had the courtesy to provide the customary bouquets for the singers and the composer. The composer was crushed by this rebuff and was heard to say: 'So I am too old, so I am not to write any more; they don't want anything else from me!' [1] But two days later, on 5th November, he was heartened by a genuine triumph when Adolf Čech conducted the complete cycle of symphonic poems, *My Fatherland*. According to Zelený this occasion could only be compared with the great day when *Libuše* was performed.

During the summer Smetana began to plan a second string quartet, but he experienced greater difficulty than at any previous time. He complained to Srb-Debrnov [2] of feeling stunned and drowsy, and he was afraid he was gradually losing his vivid musical imagination and had reached the end of his power to create original music. He told Zelený on 26th September [3] that he could no longer remember what he had written down and was obliged to re-read it, which meant he could 'scarcely write four bars a day'. He had had bronchial catarrh for several months, which often prevented him from speaking. Some-times loud talking caused such acute pain in his throat that for hours he was unable to work. Without realizing it he sometimes sang as he composed, and so loudly that his vocal organs would become com-pletely exhausted. But he complained most about the state of his nerves. In his letter to Srb-Debrnov of 9th December he said: [4]

A great change has come over me! About three weeks ago towards evening I lost my voice, that is to say the ability to express my thoughts. I could not even read what came to hand, and was unable to remember the names of people alive or dead. I just shouted 'tye-tye-tye' with long intervals in between, during which I kept my mouth open. No one knew what to do and the doctor was about to be called—it was already late in the evening—when the attack quietly came to an end and I could read again and remember all names. A few days later, after about a week, the

---

[1] V. V. Zelený; *K životopisu B. Smetany*; Bartoš, *op. cit.*

[2] Letter of 14th July 1882; Balthasar, *op. cit.*, pp. 208–9.

[3] Zelený, *op. cit.*; Bartoš, *op. cit.*

[4] Balthasar, *op. cit.*, pp. 220–1.

attack recurred in a more extreme form and I was unable to pronounce a single word. I was put to bed at once where I gradually recovered. The doctor forbade me to drink wine, beer and all spirits etc., and explained that it was due to pressure of blood on the brain and that I might easily lose my memory or even become insane. The mental exertion caused by musical invention and continual deafness without any alleviation of the aural nerves caused this strong rush of blood to the brain, which as it were became numb and unable at that time to comprehend anything. The doctor forbade me to read for more than a quarter of an hour and told me to cease all musical activity completely, unless I wished to forfeit my entire musical talent. So I must not think in terms of music, neither read through my compositions nor those of others, nor recall them to mind, even if this trouble continues for a whole year. It was high time something was done, because signs of deterioration had appeared when I was in Prague. When I was there I became dissatisfied, especially because I was beginning to detest my new compositions, which sometimes annoyed me so much that my whole body trembled. I felt cold all through the summer and my inclination to joke became rarer and rarer.

In defiance of his doctor's orders, Smetana made a little progress with his quartet and finished it off on 12th March 1883. After writing a male-voice chorus he began working on a suite of symphonic dances, *Prague Carnival*. By 14th September he had written and scored the Introduction and Polonaise (124 bars for large orchestra), but this was all he could do. In the meantime, after a long interval, he again began thinking of his proposed opera *Viola*. At this time changes were taking place in preparation for the opening of the rebuilt National Theatre. F. A. Šubert had replaced Maýr as administrative and artistic director and was establishing a more liberal regime, in consequence of which Smetana's honorarium was increased from 1,200 to 1,500 gulden and his royalties on *Libuše* from sixty to one hundred gulden. This festival opera was chosen for the opening night of the new building, which took place on 18th November.

The Umělecká beseda arranged to honour their vice-president, Dr Hostinský, on 10th October when it was announced that he had been made a university professor; Smetana made a point of being present to congratulate his friend. Those who were there could not help noticing that the composer was beginning to lose his reason. According to Zelený [1] Smetana 'described how a crowd of unknown and diverse people entered his room through the closed door, notably some beautiful and richly clothed women; he failed to understand where they came from and why they sought him out in his loneliness, and jocularly advised the ladies to go to Prague, where they would find more amusing company.' During the same evening Smetana made the following reference to *Viola*: 'I am still writing something, but I am only writing that so that people will know what goes on in the head of a musician who is in my state.'

There is further evidence of his mental unbalance in his letters. When he wrote to Srb-Debrnov on 8th January 1884 he added the following postscript: [2]

Viola! My breast swells with pride that this artistic distinction should have been meant for me! O Viola, tell those gentlemen in Prague how my soul has been moved to tears—tears! I am sending you those divine melodies from the first act so that you can enjoy those parts to your heart's content! Some turn me into—an angel! I am sending them for you to arrange as—*a string quartet!* nothing otherwise for the beginning. The numbers don't exist. It's nothing to get excited about, but will be admired! *All hail Viola!*

In a mixture of Czech and German he wrote to Srb-Debrnov in the following pathetic manner: [3] 'In the greatest haste I write to ask you to buy me twenty to thirty postage stamps, red with the large five on. I am so angry that I should like nothing better than to fire cannons into them.'

Smetana was in a melancholy mood at this time and hallucinations were frequent. When he imagined his friends and admirers were coming to visit him, he stood at the open window, bowed, and beckoned with both hands to his phantoms. A servant was constantly on guard day and night, in case he came to any harm. [4] He wrote a postcard to

[1] *Op. cit.*; Bartos, *op. cit.*

[2] Balthasar, *op. cit.*, p. 268.

[3] Facsimile in Balthasar, *op. cit.* Smetana sketched the stamps.

[4] Havlin, B., 'Trpitelský život B. Smetany', in *Čaroděj tonů* (Mladá Boleslav, 1926); Bartoš, *op. cit.*

himself on his birthday (2nd March), and then wrote on scraps of paper to Mozart, Beethoven and unknown people. Finally he had bouts of anger, he tried to escape and no longer recognized his own family. A particularly severe attack occurred on 20th April, which made it imperative to transfer him to the Prague lunatic asylum on the 23rd. While he was there he was forced to eat, but he became weaker and wasted away. His babbling speech became incomprehensible. Always restless, he would sometimes imagine he was conducting an orchestra, growling and trying to imitate the sound of the instruments as he did so. Occasionally he would emit the moaning, broken laughter of a paralytic. His sufferings ended when he died at half past four on the afternoon of 12th May 1884.[1] On the following day Dr Hlava carried out a post-mortem examination.[2]

The funeral rites were performed three days later at the Týn Church in the Old Town Square. A great crowd followed the cortège to the National Museum, where fanfares were sounded, and on to the Vyšehrad Cemetery, where Smetana was laid to rest. Dr Jan Strakatý, the vice-chairman of the Theatre Association, made the funeral oration. In a letter to Karel Havrátil, Liszt said how deeply he had been affected by his friend's death, and declared: 'He was indeed a genius.'

[1] Report by Dr Wenzel Walter; Rychnovský, *op. cit.*, p. 255.
[2] See Appendix E, p. 150.

CHAPTER VIII

PIANOFORTE MUSIC

The piano music falls into several fairly well defined categories. The dances are the most numerous, with the polkas taking pride of place. Next come the album leaves and sketches, but since some of these have titles they tend to overlap with the third group, the characteristic pieces. The concert studies, the *Allegro capriccioso*, the *Fantasia on Czech National Songs* and the transcription of Schubert's *Der Neugierige* represent a small group of virtuosic pieces, but elements of virtuosity also appear in other compositions. The Sonata in G minor is the most ambitious work from the years when Smetana was studying with Proksch. The best of the piano music testifies to the composer's keen understanding of the potentialities of his instrument, and points unequivocally towards his innate sense of artistry, his lively imagination and also his skill as an executive artist.

At the age of sixteen he was already able to write music with character, as we may see from the *Jiřinková Polka*, but familiarity with the music of Schumann, Mendelssohn and Chopin helped to give the pieces that followed more refinement and polish; by the time he wrote the *Capriccio in Mazurka Style*, the Waltz of 1844 and the *Bagatelles and Impromptus* his work had even more assurance and a greater sense of purpose. One section of the Waltz was the basis of the first duet in *The Bartered Bride*, and the *Pensée fugitive* reappeared in the incomplete *Cid-Ximena* project. It seems possible that the fresh and original 'Fairy Tale' from the *Bagatelles and Impromptus* may have given ideas to some later composers. Most of the work that Smetana did for Proksch betrays its pedagogic origin, but the G minor Sonata is in quite a different class. It required immeasurably greater concentration to compose a thirty-minute work like this than to throw off salon pieces and dances, and Smetana was surprisingly successful with the Adagio. The varied treatment that he gives to the melody each time it reappears shows considerable resource and imagination. The main material of the finale did not need very much reshaping when he used it again in the finale of his G minor Piano Trio. In the same year as the Sonata he wrote the Polka in E flat major: quite the best he had written up to that time. By the time he wrote the *Six Characteristic Pieces*, Op. 1, he was beginning to spread his wings. Each of the pieces creates a vivid musical impression, and the ideas are more fully developed than before. The canon 'In the forest' flows perfectly naturally and 'The shepherdess' has a simple charm. The portrait of 'The soldier' is full of movement, and 'Rising passion' goes through several different stages before reaching its climax.

There are two types of album leaf, the brief pieces that were written for the albums of Smetana's friends or to commemorate royal weddings, and the more extended pieces that he planned to write in every major and minor key. As in the case of Chopin's *Preludes* these were to be arranged in the order C major, A minor, G major, E minor, D major, B minor, and so on round the circle of fifths.[1] The first six were published by Kistner as Op. 2, but he was not prepared to issue any further sets. Smetana therefore abandoned his systematic order and offered miscellaneous sets of pieces to two other publishers. Hallberger published 'To Robert Schumann' and 'Wayfarer's Song', but not 'Es siedet und braust . . .', the third piece that the composer included with them to form his Op. 3.[2] Veit issued eight pieces in two volumes entitled *Sketches*, Opp. 4 and 5. Smetana composed twenty-nine album leaves, including more than one in the same key, but did not complete any pieces in C minor, F major and D minor.

These pieces, which make admirable teaching material, are simple in style and in almost every case grow out of a single musical idea. Several pieces have titles, but no clue is offered for the enigmatic piece in B minor (Op. 2, No. 6), which modulates to B flat major and D flat major. The range of mood is considerable and includes

[1] The eight *Bagatelles and Impromptus* follow a similar key plan up to C sharp minor. The *Six Characteristic Pieces* are in the major and minor keys of C, G and D.

[2] A corruption of 'Es wallet und siedet und brauset und zischt', from Schiller's poem 'Der Taucher'.

melancholy, mystery, contentment, gaiety, vivacity (Toccatina) and agitation (Relentless struggle). Here and there we notice Schuman‑nesque elements, as for instance in the syncopated melody of the B flat major piece for Countess Thun's album, the texture of Op. 2, No. 2 and the persistent rhythm of Op. 5, No. 4, yet the conceptions are Smetana's own. When the composer sent twelve of his album leaves to Clara Schumann, she was particularly pleased with 'Pre‑ludium', 'Wayfarer's Song', 'Scherzo‑Polka', 'Es siedet und braust . . .' and 'To Robert Schumann'. This last piece includes an important anticipation of a theme for *Libuše* (see p. 101).

The atttractive *Wedding Scenes*, written in 1849 for his pupil Countess Marie F. Thun at the time of her marriage to Baron L. Aerenthal, comprise a 'Wedding procession' which is a remarkable anticipation of the *slatter* of Grieg, a 'duet' representing the bride and bridegroom, and 'Wedding revels', where we encounter the striking polka used later at the beginning of *The Bartered Bride*. Smetana dedi‑cated the *Allegro capriccioso* to his friend Alexander Dreyschock. As Očadlík has pointed out, the capriciousness of this fine concert piece hinges on the equal balance of defiant and rosmarine moods. Three exceptionally contrasted pieces form *A Treasure of Melodies*. After the meditative and slightly Schumannesque 'Preludium' comes a brilliantly vital 'Capriccio', which in turn is followed by a staccato study with a pronounced Czech spirit. It was during this period that the composer felt the need to write compositions for two pianos, eight hands, for the pupils of his music school. But neither the Sonata in E minor (in one movement and on classical lines) nor the Rondo in C fulfil much more than their pedagogic purpose.

During the early 1850s Smetana showed an especial interest in polkas, and in several cases he returned to these later in order to improve and revise them. The biggest changes were made in the Polka in G minor, very possibly because the composer did not con‑sider what he had written was sufficiently characteristic of this dance. He rejected the first twenty‑eight bars and the end of the piece, and based the new polka (*Poetic Polkas*, No. 2) on the remaining twenty‑two bars, which he expanded four‑fold. In this way he retained the striking example of chromatic writing over a pedal that occurs in the earlier piece. This one is rivalled in popularity by the F sharp major Polka (*Salon Polkas*, No. 1), but all the other dances in these two sets have attractive features. The reason for rewriting the Polka in C was the irresistible attraction of his Swedish friend Fröjda Benecke. In the new version, *Vision at the Ball*, Smetana gives this jog-trot dance rather more distinction by means of an introduction based on her musical cryptogram (FEDA) and an additional touch of virtuosity. Fröjda's influence is also seen in the extremely interesting yet tantalizingly incomplete Ballad in E minor, which later provided some ideas for *Dalibor*, and also in his transcription of Schubert's sixth *Maid of the Mill* song, 'Der Neugierige', the words of which reveal his feelings towards her. Smetana keeps close to Schubert's setting, but he allows himself a little virtuosic display before the last stanza, which he then adorns with trills and other decorative features. During his Swedish period Smetana wrote the two pairs of polkas, *Memories of Bohemia*. In each case it is the second polka that shows most resource and imagination, but whereas Op. 12, No. 2 (dedicated to Fröjda) is a little repetitive, Op. 13, No. 2 (for Bettina) is a splendidly vital composition and the biggest and boldest of all his polkas.

It is natural that Smetana's indebtedness to Liszt should be conspicuous in the virtuoso pieces, but it must not be overlooked that Smetana made personal contact with Tausig and that he was familiar with the music of Hummel, Kalkbrenner, Moscheles, Thalberg, Alkan, Henselt and others. In Smetana's Concert Study in C (Scherzo study) Liszt's influence is most obvious in the lyrical sections, which provide a welcome respite after the brilliance and turbulence of the beginning. In this piece the composer displays supreme self-confidence and a splendid sense of control, and demonstrates clearly that he must have been an exceptionally able pianist. The better known concert study *On the Seashore* rather regrettably leans even more heavily on the example of Liszt, which means it is all the more predictable, and since the Swedish sea is represented in a relatively tranquil state the expressive range is limited.

Between the composition of *Wallenstein's Camp* and *Haakon Jarl* Smetana made a complete piano draft of another programmatic work, *Macbeth and the Witches*. The first part represents the answers made by the apparitions to Macbeth's three unspoken questions, the vision of the procession of the eight kings and the dance of the witches before they vanish. In the opening bars the hags are suggested by the following remarkable atonal passage:

Più moderato

The second half presents the battle between Malcolm's army and Macbeth's troops, and the proclamation of Malcolm as king. The witches' dance is akin in spirit to a *Mephisto Waltz*. The dissonance and syncopation of Macbeth's brief theme suggests him racked with mental anguish. A thrice repeated A major triad and a theme that grows out of this seem to suggest the crown. The procession of kings is represented by a D minor melody and a theme in C sharp minor seems to be associated with Malcolm. A possible reason why Smetana never scored this interesting symphonic work for orchestra is that he may have realized that Malcom's noble theme carries an inappropriate weight of tragedy.

When Smetana resumed composing for the piano after an interval of thirteen years he was quite a different person, musically speaking, from the composer of the early sixties. During this time he had written five operas and three more symphonic poems, and it is hardly necessary to add that he was not only deaf but far more mature. In the pieces of these final years he began to move out of the milieu of the salon and towards his country's folk music, and a greater intensity of musical feeling becomes apparent. The cycle of six pieces entitled *Dreams* employs modulation with greater subtlety than hitherto, a factor that seems to have led Smetana's pupil Josef Jiránek to imagine that what he regarded as 'unpleasant dissonances' were due to 'mistakes'. Smetana rebuked him for his lack of understanding. Smetana's new approach is well illustrated by the second and third pieces. 'In the salon' is a well integrated piece with a greater emotional range than one would expect, and 'In Bohemia' makes a restrained use of national elements, and ends quietly brooding on what has gone before.

Two themes are used in alternation in 'Before the castle', one strongly heroic in character and the other feminine in feeling. The second of these returns to crown the piece at its climax.[1] The cycle ends with 'Harvest home', which is based on several Czech dance rhythms including that of the *skočná*. Smetana presents a whole series of moods of peasant rejoicing and writes here with considerable skill and superb panache.

Smetana brought the art of polka composition to its most refined state in his *Czech Dances*. The four polkas in the first part are more pensive than his earlier examples, except for No. 3, which recalls the exuberance and gaiety of the past. No. 2 in A minor and No. 4 in B flat major are the most individual and show the transformation of style most clearly. Like several of the earlier polkas these are not intended to be danced to, and they are idealizations of various aspects of the dance. When after two years Smetana selected ten other dances to serve as the inspiration of the second half of this work, he again conveyed the essential spirit of each in an imaginative and rather free manner. For five of these he borrowed tunes from Erben's collection[2] and wrote his pieces around them, and in almost every case he worked elements of these melodies into the introductory bars and into later parts of the pieces, in addition to presenting them in a simple and direct manner early in each piece. The brief five-bar fragment that is the basis of 'Oves', and which differs from the Erben version, provided almost all the material needed for the third dance. 'Medvěd' includes a completely independent section suggesting the mellifluous tones of the Czech bagpipes, and 'Dupák', which is not founded on a national melody, also has a bagpipe episode.[3] Although Smetana did not draw

---

[1] The swift modulation from B minor through C minor to E flat major within two bars in the coda should be noted.

[2] K. J. Erben, *Prostonárodní české písně a říkadla s nápěvy* (Prague, 1862–4). The dances with their equivalent numbers in Erben are: 'Oves' (592), 'Medvěd' (118), 'Cibulička' (124), 'Hulán' (379) and 'Obkročák' (451).

[3] A *dupák* is a stamping dance. 'Medvěd' (the bear) is the dance known as the *bavorák*. The dances *oves* (oats), *cibulička* (little onion) and *hulán* (the lancer) take their names from the first lines of the songs. 'Slepička' means 'little hen'.

directly from folk material for his 'Furiant', this has an obvious affinity with the well-known tune 'Sedlák, sedlák', which served as his model for the dance in the second act of *The Bartered Bride*. This set of dances provides a fascinating commentary on some of the more characteristic dance types of Bohemia, ranging from the more moderately paced ones like *oves*, *cibulička* and *sousedská* to the animated and vivacious *furiant*, *dupák* and *skočná*.

CHAPTER IX

CHAMBER MUSIC

Not one of Smetana's compositions written before the autumn of
1855 provides us with any tangible evidence that he was capable of
creating music with a deep emotional content, a work that would
strike to the heart of the listener. The *Triumphal Symphony* was his
most ambitious composition, and this gave a foretaste of the composer's
monumental style which reached its climax in *Libuše*, but Smetana
needed an entirely different stimulus, the experience of deep personal
tragedy, to impel him to write the elegiac Piano Trio in G minor. It
is true that at several points and in different ways the trio bears a close
resemblance to aspects of Schumann's style and that it takes some hints
from Liszt, and also that Smetana did not write in a manner that is
wholly characteristic of himself, yet his achievement was tremendous.
At one bound he became a composer with an intensely vital message,
and he had sufficient mastery to be able to communicate this with real
conviction.

The central core of the first movement, the emotive theme announced
unaccompanied on the G string of the violin, may be recognized as
a mid-nineteenth-century variant and extension of the baroque
chromatic symbol for grief:

This idea is superbly extended by the piano with the support of the other instruments. The second theme in B flat major for the cello momentarily offers a little balm, and when the piano pushes the tonality upwards by semitones there is an added sweetness. A new rhythmic rising theme for the piano briefly provides an unexpectedly cheer-ful note, but Šourek's suggestion that this represents a happy recollec-tion of four-year-old Bedřiška's exceptional musical talent does not carry complete conviction. This theme starts from C major and moves rapidly through sharp keys and back to B flat major, where the cello theme returns in triumphant form. The development of this movement is particularly intense until the climax is reached, after which it dis-integrates and leads in a deliberately inconclusive manner to the re-capitulation. The mood of tragedy is strengthened by the final stretto.

References are made to the first movement in the plaintive inter-mezzo. This has two Alternativi in major keys, the first of which includes typical Schumannesque signs, and the second being a majes-tic episode with reminders of archaic sequences. After this movement Smetana provided a highly animated finale which takes as its starting point the first eighty-seven bars of the Molto vivace of his Piano Sonata. The basic theme is of the same primitive type as the second theme in the finale of Schubert's E flat Trio, and it has obvious associa-tions with the cimbalom. A similar theme is found in Dvořák's String Quintet, Op. 97. In Smetana's movement a noble cello theme, suggestive of the composer's grief, twice interrupts the vivacious mood and finally gives rise to a funeral march, and here the triplet octaves from the beginning of the movement reappear to suggest a muffled drum.

Smetana gave the following description of his String Quartet in E minor, *Z mého života* (From my life), in a letter to J. Srb-Debrnov on 12th April 1878:[1]

I had no intention of writing any quartet according to the customary for-

[1] Balthasar, *op. cit.*, pp. 129–32.

mulas, on which I worked sufficiently as a young student of music theory, methods with which I am thoroughly familiar and have mastered. For me the design of each composition depends upon its subject. And so this quartet brought about by itself such form as it possesses. I wanted namely to represent in sound the course of *my life.*

1st movement: love of art in my youth, my *romantic mood*, the unspoken longing for something which I could not name or imagine clearly, and also a warning as it were of my future misery ♪♪ and of the long note sounding in the finale ♪♪♪ etc., arising from that beginning. It is the fatal high-pitched whistling in my ear which in 1874 announced my deafness. Since it was so *fatal* to me this little freak made me suffer.

2nd movement: Quasi Polka, bringing reminders of the happy times of my youth, when as a composer I strewed the young world with *dance pieces*, and was known everywhere as an enthusiastic dancer, etc. Trio: Meno vivo, D flat major . . . in this section I depicted in sound reminders of the aristocratic circles in which I lived for a long time . . .

3rd movement: Largo sostenuto, recalling the happiness of my first love for the girl who later became my faithful wife.[1]

4th movement: knowledge of how to make use of the element of *national music*, joy at the outcome of following this path, until the ominous interruption and catastrophe, *the beginning of deafness*; a glance towards the sad future, then comes a brief sign of improvement, but a reminder from the very beginning of my love [of art] results finally in a sensation of *pain.*

Despite what Smetana said, he retained the basic four-movement classical scheme and wrote the first and last movements in sonata form. The opening movement's first subject and transition are omitted in the recapitulation, yet this movement is more orthodox than 'Reveries, Passions' in Berlioz's *Fantastic Symphony*. A programmatic string quartet on the other hand was virtually without precedent.[2] The same letter

[1] Letters to F. A. Urbánek and O. Kopecký add some details, including: 'Struggle with unfavourable destiny to achieve the final aim.'

[2] Being an arrangement, Haydn's *Seven Last Words* for string quartet is a special case.

provides us with some additional information. The long, passionate viola theme at the beginning represents 'Fate's summons to take part in life's combat'. Smetana visualized the gentle and melodious G major theme which follows (and which is recalled in the finale) as 'affection for romance in music and love', and he explained that 'romance in love' implied a 'melancholy and passionate musical style'. The fanfare-like viola theme in the scherzo reminded Smetana of a post-horn.

The G major theme just mentioned is subtly transformed when it becomes the codetta theme, and the development that follows in its wake is powerful. The second movement's trio in D flat major is exceptionally original and particularly fascinating, but to Antonín Bennewitz and his colleagues it provided insuperable problems. The Largo sostenuto, which is based on a pair of melodies, is full of imaginative scoring and is harmonically interesting. At its climax the instruments proclaim the main theme in full chords in C major, a device that Dvořák copied in his G major Quartet. The chromatic harmony at the end of Smetana's movement also attracted Dvořák's attention, for a similar chord (B natural, E flat, F and G over a tonic pedal A flat) is seen in the first movement of his String Quartet in A flat (see illustration on page 69). The scoring of the beginning of Dvořák's F major Quartet clearly stems from the opening of *From My Life*.[1] Smetana's finale rushes on gaily and unrestrained until the dramatic and tragic conclusion is reached, and here the falling fifth takes on its full and fatal significance.

Smetana was far less explicit about his second String Quartet in D minor, but in a letter to V. V. Zelený he remarked:[2]

> ... I am writing a quartet in defiance of the doctors. The new quartet continues from where the first one ended, after the catastrophe. It introduces the swirl of music of a person who has lost his hearing. As for that, no one can imagine how the thoughts of a deaf person fly from him. If I don't write them down immediately I can't remember them, and yet I used to be renowned for my prodigious memory.

[1] Dvořák took part in the first private performance of Smetana's quartet at Srb-Debrnov's home during April 1878.

[2] Letter of 9th March 1883; Šourek, *Komorní skladby B. Smetany* (Prague, 1945), p. 49.

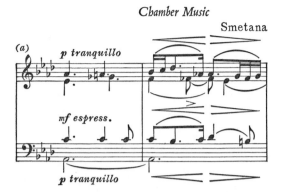

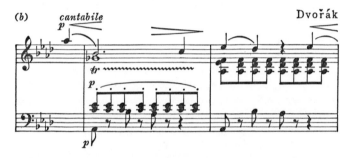

During the previous summer he told Srb-Debrnov:[1]

I have finished the first movement of the quartet, but I am in rather a quandary about its style; it is quite unusual in form and difficult to follow, as if the whole movement was the product of whim, so it seems to me it will present great difficulties to the players—that is the consequence of my miserable existence.

[1] Letter of 14th July 1882; Balthasar, *op. cit.*, p. 209.

But ten months later he reported to Srb-Debrnov:[1] '. . . the quartet begins to establish itself, so that in any case I am sending it to be published, for it is good and has melodic moments full of feeling and innovations.'

Essentially the opening movement is based upon two themes, the first a fiery unison motif in triplets, which may suggest the extreme frustration caused by the composer's deafness, and the second a slower yearning theme in F major, which in its more animated form may symbolize his rising spirits at the discovery that he could find solace in composition. Since the first theme is pushed into the background and the movement ends peacefully (in F major, not D minor), there is some internal evidence to support this theory. The second movement, a delightful syncopated polka with a gracious triple-time trio, is derived from a twenty-bar fragment written more than thirty years earlier and inexplicably left incomplete. This eighteen-minute quartet, written a few bars at a time under the most trying physical conditions, is unpredictable, full of contrasts and is sometimes quirkish. Yet it is clearly the work of a man who remained exceptionally sensitive and self-critical, and who still retained his love for 'romance in music' and possessed a deep understanding of musical beauty.

Like the *Czech Dances* for piano that preceded them, the two pieces for violin and piano, *Z domoviny* (From the homeland), testify to Smetana's interest in folk music. The second in particular approaches so closely to the spirit of his country's folk-song and dance that we might be tempted to think that actual folk material is used. The C major tune has an obvious kinship with the Slovak melody *Prídi ty, šuhajko!* Both of the pieces display a characteristic blend of melancholy and gaiety, but the second bubbles over irrepressibly at the change from G minor to G major and the *skoký*-type [2] dance commences.

[1] Letter of 24th May 1883; Balthasar, *op. cit.*, p. 244.

[2] This is František Bonuš's general term for the men's leaping dances of Moravia, Slovakia and elsewhere.

CHAPTER X

ORCHESTRAL WORKS

The *Triumphal Symphony*, written in commemoration of Franz Josef's marriage, shows how much Smetana had progressed since composing the Overture in D major, or *Festive Overture*, of four years earlier. The structural weakness of the overture was most conspicuous. The symphony, on the other hand, is far more assured, much more typical of the composer, and is more imaginatively scored, notably in the passage for sustained bassoons and horns, with a staccato background for second violins, that occurs in the first movement. The first two phrases of Haydn's *Emperor's Hymn* are heard shortly before the recapitulation in this movement. The hymn is far more prominent in the Largo maestoso, where it is transformed into triple time and serves to crown the movement when the tonic key returns. It is not heard in the scherzo, but is magnificently arrayed for its majestic entry at the end of the finale. The scherzo is like neither Beethoven nor Mendelssohn, but is swift and light with occasional *furiant*-type cross rhythms, whereas the trio is more earthy, suggesting a dance of peasants. The length of the work, and especially of the slow movement, is a handicap, but the scherzo is worth playing on its own.

Smetana outlined the plan of his first symphonic poem, *Richard III*, in a letter to Liszt:[1]

It consists of one movement and its emphasis inclines roughly towards the action of the tragedy: the attainment of the chosen aim after overcoming all obstacles, the triumph and finally the downfall of the hero. . . . The

theme in the basses

[1] Letter of 24th October 1858; Teige, *Příspěvky k životopisu a umělecké činnosti mistra Bedřicha Smetany II, Dopisy Smetanovy* (Prague, 1896), pp. 17–18. Smetana misquoted the Richard theme.

represents the character of the hero himself, who is active throughout, and

this one:  stands for his antagonists.

Much later when writing to Srb-Debrnov he said:[1]

> Those who know Shakespeare's Richard III may imagine the whole tragedy just as they like during the course of the music. To enumerate in detail all the scenes and the whole action is impossible, and you must not expect that from me! But I can say this, that in the very first bar I present a kind of musical characterization of *Richard's personality*, and this main theme in all manner of different forms predominates throughout the entire work. Before the end I have tried to give a musical portrayal of that terrible *dream* in *Richard's* tent on the night before the battle, in which ghosts of all those he murdered prophesy his doom on the following day. It ends with Richard's downfall. In the middle of the work comes Richard's triumph as king, followed by his gradual decline until the end.

With this outline before us there is no difficulty in identifying the main features of the work, but further points may be mentioned. In this predominantly Maestoso composition, there is a conspiratorial *Più allegro vivo* before Richard gains the crown; a new motif, derived from the latter part of the basic Richard theme, is used in the dream (Più mosso); and the antagonists' theme is combined with and over-powers the Richard theme in the final battle. As Roger Fiske has pointed out, Smetana's portrayal of the misshapen king's limp is brilliant:

[Maestoso, quasi Andante]

---

[1] Letter of 14th February 1881; Balthasar, *op. cit.*, p. 168.

Since the two principal themes include the same strongly rhythmic motif, this figure tends to be overworked. The influence of Liszt is seen in the antagonists' theme and also in the general conception of the work, but Smetana's increasing mastery in symphonic composition is far more important.

The next symphonic poem, *Wallenstein's Camp*, was intended originally to be an overture to Schiller's play. The bustle of colourful life in a military encampment, where Schiller observed clear signs of the General's criminal lust for power, suited Smetana better than the portrayal of tragic heroes like Richard III and Haakon Jarl, but instead of following Schiller in making the camp cosmopolitan, he fastened on to the fact that it lay near Pilsen and gave it a distinctly Czech character. Since he took only one scene directly from Schiller —the dancing, followed by the Capuchin friar's denunciation of the rogues around him—it became necessary to follow this with two scenes of his own. The work therefore is in one continuous movement, yet has similarities with a four-movement symphony with the following scheme: I. Crowd scene; II. (Scherzo) Dancing and friar's harangue (followed by a short recapitulation of I); III. (Slow movement) The camp asleep; IV. Reveille and march.

Just as the two motifs in the first part are fundamentally the same, so in the second part the themes are transformations of the bagpipe tune (a). Schiller's Capuchin, who assumed the form of Fra Melitone in *Un ballo in maschera*,[1] is grotesquely represented by three trombones and a tuba (b); he is mocked by the crowd (treble instruments, and

[1] Julian Budden has kindly drawn my attention to the following passage referring to the friar in Verdi's letter of 24th March 1849: '. . . persino un frate che predica alla maniera più comica e deliziosa del mondo.' (F. Abbiati, *Giuseppe Verdi*, vol. ii, 1959.)

later in imitation by bassoons and bass strings), and when he departs the crowd exults (c):

By the time he wrote *Wallenstein's Camp* Smetana had recovered from the overwhelming experience of his visit to Liszt in September 1857,[1] and in consequence it was possible for him to make this a more impressive and personal work than *Richard III*.

A year before his death, Smetana wrote to Adolf Čech on the subject of his third symphonic poem, *Haakon Jarl*, but his bad memory led him to give a such garbled version of the plot of Öhlenschläger's drama that his letter (7th May 1883) will mislead those who turn to it for guidance on the music. Briefly, the historical facts are as follows.

---

[1] Smetana's letter to Liszt of 24th October 1858 stresses the powerful impression his friend's music made on him, and states his firm belief in the sacred truth of Liszt's views on progress in art.

Having murdered Harald Graafeld, Earl Haakon of Lade seized power in A.D. 970 and ruled most of Norway tyrannically for twenty-five years. Olaf Tryggvessön (Olaf the Saint) spent his boyhood in exile, and defeated Haakon when he invaded his fatherland in 995. After being proclaimed king, Olaf converted Norway to Christianity, but his reign was cut short by his death in the year 1000.

Smetana's sympathies lay with Earl Haakon (who was finally slain by one of his own followers) and also with the people, who according to Öhlenschläger were shocked by Haakon's cruel and unprincipled behaviour. He was prejudiced against Olaf, who is presented in a very favourable light in the play. The symphonic poem falls into three parts. The first part serves as an introduction (Andante energico) in which the lamentations of the people and a hint of Christian singing are heard, followed by Olaf's march-like theme played by the full orchestra; after some harp cadenzas Earl Haakon is presented as a noble figure and there is a further reference to Olaf. The second part (Allegro molto—Maestoso grandioso) probably represents the invasion and certainly the battle and victory of Olaf, which gives the people new heart. The final section (Andante religioso) is a hymn of thanksgiving, at the end of which there are some last thoughts on the fallen hero.

Practically all the smaller compositions that followed these symphonic poems—a Shakespearean march, pieces for *tableaux vivants* and overtures for puppet plays—emphasize Smetana's interest in the stage. The little overture to *Doctor Faust* is scored for two horns, trombone, triangle, bass drum, strings and piano. It is a polished little drama in itself. At the beginning the stiff and angular movements of puppets are suggested, and a fugal exposition follows. When the climax is reached we become fully aware of Mephistopheles's power over his victim. The *March for the Shakespearean Festival* is written on a grand scale and relies on the intensification of rhythm to drive it onwards towards its climax.

Just as Smetana was putting the final touches to his national epic *Libuše*, he conceived the idea of composing another national monument, the cycle of six symphonic poems, *Má vlast* (My Fatherland). At one time he hoped to include among the chosen subjects

Říp (the hill from which the legendary Grandfather Čech surveyed the lands of Bohemia and chose them for his people), *Lipany* (scene of a massacre during the Hussite wars) and *Bílá Hora* (the White Mountain, where the Bohemian knights were defeated by the Hapsburgs in the fatal battle in 1620), but these were not composed. The cycle in its final form presents a crosssection of Czech history and legend and impressions of its scenery, and as a whole conveys vividly to us Smetana's view of the ethos and greatness of his nation. It is a unified work and makes its greatest impact when heard as a whole. The following pertinent remarks have been made about it by František Bartoš:[1]

. . . it was directly in the spirit and ideological grandeur of the opera 'Libuše' that 'My Fatherland' was written. Both works are ideologically similar in their glorification of the country and its people, dictated by the period of their origin. We must not forget that it was the time of the culmination of the active struggle of the politically oppressed Czech nation for independence and the attainment of a full cultural and political life which had been waged for almost a hundred years. 'My Fatherland' and 'Libuše' are direct symbols of that consummating national struggle. Their stressed national tendencies, resulting naturally from such circumstances, their conflicts and ardent optimism, indicating a great future for the nation, are the reasons why both works are fully understood and appreciated only by Smetana's countrymen. They have both become national *sacrosancta* to which the whole nation turns in times of crises. For this reason too a foreigner can comprehend only with difficulty the specific ideological atmosphere of these most monumental of Smetana's works. Similarly it is also the reason why just this most essential feature of Smetana's creative genius escapes him, and why, chiefly under the influence of his impression of the most successful of Smetana's works, 'The Bartered Bride', his general picture of the composer is far more onesided than is merited by actual fact.

Smetana gave an authentic outline of the content of the six symphonic poems in a letter to the publisher F. A. Urbánek at the end of May 1879. It is given here in full:[2]

Introduction to the Collected Edition score.
[2] Introduction to Collected Edition score; Bartoš, *op. cit.*

I. Vyšehrad.

The harps of the seers begin; a seer's song [1] about the events at Vyšehrad, of the glory, splendour, tournaments, battles, up to the final decline and ruin. The work ends on an elegiac note (Nachgesang der Barden).

II. Vltava.

The work depicts the course of the Vltava, beginning from the two small sources, the cold and warm Vltava, the joining of both streams into one, then the flow of the Vltava through forests and across meadows, through the countryside where gay festivals are just being celebrated; by the light of the moon a dance of water nymphs; on the nearby cliffs proud castles, mansions and ruins rise up; the Vltava swirls in the St John's rapids, flows in a broad stream as far as Prague, the Vyšehrad appears, and finally the river disappears in the distance as it flows majestically into the Elbe.

III. Šárka.

This work does not represent the countryside but action, the legend of the maiden Šárka. The composition opens with a portrait of the enraged girl, who swears vengeance on the entire male sex because of her lover's infidelity. At a distance is heard the arrival of Ctirad and his armour-bearers, who come to humiliate and punish the maidens. From afar they hear the cry (feigned) of a maiden bound to a tree. On seeing her Ctirad is struck by her beauty, falls passionately in love with her and frees her. With a prepared potion she cheers and intoxicates Ctirad and the armour-bearers, who fall asleep. The signal of a horn summons the maidens from their distant hiding place; they rush out to commit their bloodthirsty act. The horror of a mass slaughter, the fury of Šárka's revenge satiated—that is the end of the work.

IV. From Bohemia's Fields and Forests.

This is a general impression of feelings on seeing the Czech countryside. Here on all sides fervent singing, both cheerful and melancholy, resounds from forest and field. The woodlands—in a horn solo—and the merry fertile Elbe lowlands, and other parts besides, all give praise. Everyone may interpret this work as he pleases; the poet has a clear field before him, but must of course consider the work in detail.

---

[1] Smetana added in brackets the German word 'Bardengesang'.

V. Tábor. Motto: 'Ye who are God's warriors!'

The whole structure of the work derives from this majestic song. At the main seat [of the Hussites]—at Tábor—this hymn certainly resounded most mightily and most frequently. The work also depicts resolute will, victorious battles, perseverance, and stubborn inflexibility with which the composition ends. It is not possible to analyse it in detail, but in general it encompasses the glory and fame of the Hussite wars and the invincible spirit of the Hussites.

VI. Blaník.

This is a continuation of the preceding work, *Tábor*. After their defeat the Hussite heroes took refuge in Blaník Mountain and waited in a heavy slumber for the moment when they would come to the help of their country. So those same motifs as in Tábor serve in Blaník as the foundation of the structure: 'Ye who are God's warriors!' On the basis of this melody (of the Hussite principle) the resurrection of the Czech nation, its future happiness and glory, unfold. This victorious hymn in the form of a march concludes the composition, and thus the whole cycle of symphonic poems, 'My Fatherland'. In this work there is also a short idyll, as a little intermezzo, a sketch of the situation of Blaník: a young shepherd boy shouts and plays (a shawm) and the echo answers him.

The similarity of content between *Vyšehrad* and *Libuše* is extremely significant. In the symphonic poem the seers fortell the castle's 'glory, splendour, tournaments, battles, up to the final decline and ruin', and in the opera Libuše sees visions of the great figures of her nation's history, and she prophesies a glorious future for her people. In addition to this Helfert drew attention [1] to the fact that one of the motifs that form the basis of *Vyšehrad*, (b), is identical with a passage in the opera at the moment when Radovan is conveying Libuše's command to Přemysl; that at dawn, mounted on a white charger, he shall be at the glorious *Vyšehrad portal* to become the Princess's consort. (The italicized words are set to this motif and only the harmonic support and time signature differ.) The main Vyšehrad motif (a) appears to be an ennobled version of the rising and falling fourth in (b):

[1] 'Motiv Smetanova Vyšehradu', in *Smetana*, vol. 27 (Prague, 1917); reprinted in V. Helfert, *O Smetanovi* (Prague, 1950), pp. 50–69.

In the battle section, motif (a) is used in a descent by whole tones and in imitation, as shown in (c). This passage is given considerable dramatic power when heard again as the castle falls. During the elegiac conclusion the composer's thoughts dwell on the former glory

of Vyšehrad. Smetana placed *Vyšehrad* first in order, because it provides the foundation on which the entire cycle of symphonic poems
was created. For more than eighty years now the lofty site of the
Vyšehrad fortress above the Vltava, so rich in legend, has been the
burial ground for Bohemia's most illustrious sons.

The score of Smetana's best-known and deservedly popular orchestral composition, *Vltava*, supplements the composer's description of
the work given above. The flutes in the opening bars represent the
first source of the river, and the second source is suggested a few bars
later by a downward moving figure for clarinets. In the forest section
a hunt is in progress, and the polka that follows indicates a rustic
wedding. The two Vyšehrad motifs, (a) and (b), are easily recognized.
The possible origin of Vltava's principal melody has been the subject
of much speculation. In the form in which it first appears, in E
minor, it resembles but also differs from the Swedish song *Ack
Värmeland, du sköna*, which was adapted from the Dutch song *O
Nederland! let op u saeck*.[1] Smetana was very familiar with this well-
known Swedish tune. When the melody becomes major towards the
end of the symphonic poem it betrays an obvious family likeness to
songs such as 'Ah, vous dirai-je, maman' and 'Twinkle, twinkle
little star', but the repetition of the third and fourth bars here is a
characteristic of western and southern Slav countries and of Germany.
In this form Smetana's melody comes within reasonable distance of
the Moravian 'Vyletěla holuběnka ze skály', the Slovene 'Ženil výr
se z jara' and the German 'Fuchs! du hast die Gans gestohlen',
but it is even closer to the Czech nursery rhyme 'Kočka, lese dírou,
pes oknem'. Smetana was undoubtedly influenced by some of these
traditional tunes, but his *Vltava* theme, which is in twelve-eight time,
not four-four like all the tunes that it resembles, has greater sophisti-
cation than any of them.[2]

In contrast with the enchantingly lyrical picture of nature that is
presented in *Vltava*, *Šárka* is an example of romantic blood and

---

[1] It was published in Valerius's posthumous collection *Nederlandsche
Gedenckclanck* (1626).

[2] J. Racek, *Motiv Vltavy* (Olomouc, 1944). Unpublished paper by H.
Bím.

thunder.[1] Smetana handled this subject with great assurance and controlled fecundity. His first section gives an intensely realistic impression of Šárka's rage, and the drinking scene is gay and vital. Šárka's interrelated themes—they include a stepwise descent of a third —depict her contrasting moods. A mournful clarinet suggests her feigned wailing, and Ctirad responds to this in a recitative for cellos, formed from his personal theme. The love scene reminds us of one of Smetana's favourite works, Berlioz's *Romeo and Juliet*, and the drink-ing scene gives a foretaste of the roistering of Lukaš in *The Kiss*. The snoring of the revellers is amusingly suggested by low Cs on a bassoon, and shortly before the end the dying Ctirad's theme is heard on unison trombones, sounding, as Zich points out, like 'a superhuman roar'.[2]

Smetana has invited us to seek our own interpretation of *From Bohemia's Fields and Forests*. The first section (Molto moderato) of this continuous four-part structure is in G minor and major, and seems to invoke impressions of a broad sweep of countryside teeming with life, followed by songs sad and gay. The second section (Allegro) begins in A minor with a delightful fugue on a long and somewhat chro-matic subject, which alternates with a broad melody in F major (clarinets and horns), D flat major (woodwind and horns) and A major (full orchestra). This must therefore be the forest section, and here the quiet fugue conjures up the mysterious forest life, and most probably the elusive wood sprites. The 'merry fertile Elbe lowlands' are suggested by the next section, which works back towards the tonic key and is almost all in polka rhythm. With so much dancing and Smetana's reference to the fertility of this area, Zich may well be right in thinking Smetana had harvest home in mind. Finally comes an animated coda (Più mosso, and later Presto) in which earlier themes return and one of these is greatly enlivened.

Apart from the forest section, this work stems entirely from the two fundamental musical ideas presented at the beginning, and which

[1] Janáček and Fibich both composed operas on this subject. After Dvořák had toyed with the libretto by Zeyer, Janáček misguidedly set this without first obtaining the author's permission.
[2] O. Zich, *Symfonické básně Smetanovy*, 2nd edn (Prague, 1949), p. 124.

are themselves interrelated. The first of these appears initially in the forms (a) and (b), and subsequently it becomes the basis of the polka (c):

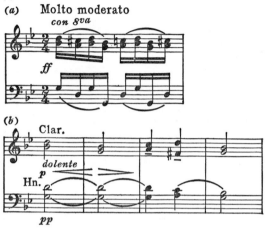

(a) **Molto moderato**

(b) **Clar.**

The second theme, the 'gay song' (d), is merged with the polka in the form (e) and reappears in the coda as (f):

(d) [**Molto moderato**]

Ob.

p espressivo

(e) **Cl.**

p

espressivo dolce

(f) **Più mosso**

Since the third section is based almost entirely on material from the first section, even though in modified form, the overall design is ternary with a coda. From several points of view this is a masterly composition.

As Smetana pointed out, the last two symphonic poems form a pair; but whereas in *Tábor* the famous Hussite chorale, *Kdož jste Boží bojovníci!*, is usually presented fragmented but unchanged, in *Blaník* it is treated rather more freely and is generally reserved for climactic points, so that it makes a far stronger impact. The complete chorale is shown here:

Ye who are God's warriors and subject to His law,
Pray for God's help and put your trust in Him,
So that finally with Him you will still be victorious.

The two complete statements of the chorale in *Tábor* rise like monoliths. Before, between and after these utterances the bracketed motifs from the first and third portions of the melody (A and C) are insisted upon or worked into the texture. The second portion (B) is scarcely used, but is played by clarinets and bassoons a few bars before the chorale is first heard as a whole, and it returns in the middle of the composition. C provides the material for the middle portion of the work and A is the basis of the beginning and the end.[1] Smetana was thinking of the first bar of the chorale when he spoke of 'stubborn inflexibility'.

With the help of Smetana's notes there seems very little doubt about his intentions in *Blaník*. In the first bars the Hussite warriors feel crushed by their defeat, and almost immediately they begin filing into the mountain. Their theme here is derived from the first part of A, and motif (x) is conspicuous. The shepherd interlude follows, and even here (x) is present, but changed to a falling fifth. The Più mosso must surely represent the distress and suffering of the people, and the Meno mosso the re-emergence of the Hussites. This latter is based on a triplet version of their theme when seeking refuge, suggesting their revived spirit of optimism. It is significant that the march grows out of C, the reason being that the words sung to this part of the chorale focus directly upon the ultimate victory. The march increases in power and even for a while turns into a dance. When the climax is reached A is combined with the two *Vyšehrad* motifs, (a) and (b).

This symphonic poem, in many ways so characteristic of the composer's work, includes two very different facets of his style. One is seen in the bustling type of theme, in continuous quavers or triplets, which we encounter in some of the operas and elsewhere. The other is far more important, and is apparent in the majesty and heroic spirit of this work. *Blaník* is certainly a splendid crown to Smetana's monumental cycle.

More than a year before his death, when the composer wrote his second String Quartet, it was clear that he wished to renounce the principles of classical form. Already at that time he admitted that he was only able to work for very short periods, and that he forgot afterwards what he had written. The Introduction and Polonaise of his projected *Prague Carnival*, all that he managed to compose of this orchestral suite, was written after the quartet, and shows some signs of the difficulties against which he was fighting. It should be noted, however, that for his main theme he turned to a sketch he had made

[1] Smetana's scheme is: A B(4 bars) Chorale C B(3 bars) C A(with references to C) Chorale A. Here the letters 'A' and 'C' represent motivic use of those portions of the melody.

twenty-five years earlier. It is important to realize that the extreme modulations in bars 35–42 are not the wild fancy of a composer who was losing his grip, but stem almost without alteration from that sketch.[1] Smetana had a remarkable gift for giving his compositions a natural sense of growth, partly by his skill in effecting transitions from one section to another, and partly by his ability to see his work as a whole. But here he appears either to be losing his skill, or alternatively rather unwisely renouncing his gifts. The work gives the impression of being too sectional; there is rather too much musical material for a composition of only a hundred and twenty-four bars, and the sense of thematic unity does not seem sufficiently strong. Although this is only a part of the work he was planning, this was the last composition that he completed.

[1] Smetana sketched forty-six bars on 14th March 1858. Bars 15–16, 22–32 and 35–46 of the Introduction and Polonaise derive directly from the sketch, which is published in facsimile in *Zápisník motivů B. Smetany* (Prague, 1942).

CHAPTER XI

CHORAL MUSIC AND SONG

Most of Smetana's choral music was written for male voice choir, a medium that was very popular at the time. The evenings were social occasions, and every singer made sure he had a well-filled mug of beer under his seat. Smetana's first setting of Jan z Hvězdy's *Czech Song* is entirely different from the two later versions. It was composed a year before the famous Prague Hlahol choral society was founded, and remains an enigma. The score is clearly marked for divided tenors and basses, and the pitch range of the first tenors is from the E flat above middle C to the B flat one and a half octaves higher. It does not make musical sense if the tenor parts are transposed down an octave. The passage in *To Robert Schumann* which the composer used much later in *Libuše* (see p. 101) occurs at the end of *Czech Song* in a form that is much closer to the Přemysl motif.

Like most of Smetana's choral music, *The Three Riders* and *The Renegade* are patriotic works. *The Three Riders*, for three solo voices and male voice choir, tells of the return from Constance of the envoys of the Czech nobility bearing the news of the martyrdom of Jan Hus, and it ends with a panegyric of the great Bohemian religious reformer. The sense of J. V. Jahn's poem is vividly conveyed in Smetana's dynamic setting. *The Renegade* is a bitter denunciation of those who betray their country, and concludes with a promise that the raven will have a dainty morsel. This is an antiphonal work for double male voice choir, and even if the concluding section is overlong it is most striking and powerful. A little later the composer wrote a rather similar alternative setting for four male soloists and choir, but the double choir version is preferable. These deeply felt and vital compositions would make welcome additions to the male voice choir repertory. *Farming* is less enterprising and original than these two works, but is well written for its medium. It describes in turn the ploughing and sowing, the harvesting and the threshing, and finally praises the farmer as a patriot. The brief *Ceremonial Chorus* was written to commemorate the early death of Smetana's friend Karel Havlíček.

Smetana excelled himself when he wrote his biggest work for male voice choir, the setting of Hálek's *Song of the Sea.* In this he presents in an animated and realistic fashion a succession of five scenes from life at sea: the bustle of activity at the port; the sadness of departure; the jovial atmosphere on board; the stimulating challenge of the boundless ocean and the elements; and the rousing welcome that greets the seamen when they land. The work should be regarded as a miniature choral drama. Some lusty singing in F major in the third part is followed by a memorable moment: the sensation of bliss caused by the rocking motion is expressed by this typically Czech passage sung in a whisper in A major:

We can detect the influence of some Czech dance rhythms in this work, but whenever a more thoughtful spirit is needed this is suggested convincingly.

In all three settings of poems by Srb-Debrnov composed during his last years, Smetana's sensitivity to words and mood is apparent. In *Dedication* his imagination was fired by the fourth stanza which presents the thought that new truths are within reach. *Our Song* reflects the remarkably optimistic spirit of the suffering composer, but also gives some indication that at last he was losing his power to conceive a work as a unity. The three part-songs for female voices were written a little earlier, for Ferdinand Heller's collection of music for schools. *Return of the Swallows* is charming, and there is an attractive tinge of sadness in *The Sun Sets Behind the Mountain*, but the piano accompaniment of these polished trifles has unfortunately been lost.

When Smetana reset *Czech Song* for mixed voices in 1868 he gave the second stanza, with its references to maidens, flowers and love, to women's voices, and instinctively turned to polka rhythms. To balance this the third stanza, accompanied by pictorial representations of branches swaying in the wind, is sung by the men. When providing an orchestral accompaniment ten years later, it was unnecessary to alter the choral parts,[1] but when the Maestoso returns in the fourth part, Smetana inserted single bars for the orchestra to add emphasis to the incisive choral ejaculations during their final exhortation. He also added a thematically related orchestral prelude and introductory bars before each part. The work originated in the interval between composition of *Dalibor* and *Libuše* and recalls their fervent national spirit, especially in the opening chorus and splendid final peroration. This cantata ranks high among Smetana's choral music.

Smetana had no particular incentive to write songs for voice and piano and left only a handful of examples. Since the earliest songs are settings of German poems, and the only songs to Czech words are the strophic unison *Song of Freedom* (1848), the song for Bozděch's tragedy *Baron Goertz* (1867) and the five Hálek *Evening Songs* (1879), he never experienced declamation problems in song composition similar to those that plagued him for a while in choral composition and in opera. The first German songs are student compositions which have no genuine individuality, but were valuable essays exploring

[1] A series of consecutive fifths result from changes made in the third part.

the possibilities of song writing. But by the time he set Rückert's *Liebesfrühling* (1853) he had a better appreciation of the value of modulation and a much surer sense of purpose.

Some of the *Evening Songs* had already been set by Fibich (1871) and Dvořák (1876) before Smetana became interested in composing them. By that time he had completed all except one of his operas. The vocal line in the songs resembles that found in the works for the stage, and in the first two songs the piano proves to be a poor substitute for the orchestra; we miss the sustained sound of strings, woodwind and horns. The first of these two songs is the finer, partly because of its greater flexibility of phrase and the greater eloquence of the voice part. The words of the poem: 'Honour him who knows how to play on the golden strings', obviously appealed to the composer. Unrequited love is the subject of the third song, which has a telling accompaniment and rises to an impressive climax at the words: 'And with sorrow I continually recognize that my weeping is not the end.' The final dominant chords remain unresolved. The brief fourth song starts off as a gay polka, but shadows fall and it ends with a rueful reminder of the beginning. This short cycle ends with an ardent love song, written with all sincerity, and yet it follows a well-worn pattern in which other composers have been more successful. It is regrettable that Smetana's last song was not a more personal utterance.

CHAPTER XII

OPERA (I)

FROM 'THE BRANDENBURGERS' TO 'LIBUŠE'

When Smetana first resolved to compose a national opera the dice were loaded heavily against him. Škroup's operas were useless as models, Skuherský's four-act heroic opera *Vladimír, God's Chosen One* was still unknown to him, and foreign operas, although useful, had a strictly limited value. His greatest assets appear to have been his intense interest in drama and his personal experience of composing symphonic music with a dramatic content. It would be absurd to claim that by writing three or four symphonic poems a man qualifies himself for writing an opera, yet paradoxically that is about the only preparatory work that Smetana ever did. Up to that time he had written very few vocal works and hardly any with a Czech text. He was still struggling with the language, and was feeling his way in the dark for another reason: there were still no generally accepted rules for Czech prosody. It is little wonder that he was not sure of the declamation in his first three operas. Once it is realized what he was up against, it comes as a surprise that *The Brandenburgers in Bohemia* was a success rather than a flop. It is certainly true that the subject was designed to stimulate patriotic fervour, but the quality of Smetana's music was the decisive factor. It is far from being a perfect work, but it represents a highly significant first step on the road to the creation of a Czech national operatic repertory.

The action of *The Brandenburgers* takes place in 1279, during the time when Bohemia was occupied by the army of Burgrave Otto V of Brandenburg. After Přemysl Otakar II was slain in battle by Rudolf, King of the Romans, his widow appointed Otto as regent, because she was confident he would drive out the hated Hapsburgs. But she did not foresee how his mercenaries would behave, nor that he would have the audacity to imprison the rightful heir to the throne. Rudolf rewarded Otto for this treachery by giving him mandatory powers over Bohemia for five years. The oppressed and starving peasantry loathed not only the foreign troops, but also the wealthy German burgesses and merchants who were lining their own pockets instead of serving the country. Sabina took this situation as the foundation for his libretto and wove upon it a fictitious plot in which Jíra, a truant serf who becomes king of the rebellious peasants, accuses the Burgess Tausendmark of abducting the Mayor of Prague's three daughters with the assistance of Brandenburg soldiers. Jíra is condemned to die, but the sentence is commuted to imprisonment thanks to the intervention of Junoš, a knight who is in love with the eldest daughter, Ludiše. When Tausendmark's perfidy is unmasked, Jíra is exonerated and granted emancipation. Finally the people shout: 'Long live the truth! Long live our rights! Long live the protectors of our glorious homeland!' This plot has some naïvities but it gave Smetana many opportunities.

When it was appropriate the composer relied on a characteristic figure or motif to provide a suitable mood and also a sense of unity to a subsection of the opera. The longest and most important of these sections is the court scene, where a solemn dotted rhythm in the bass and an upward-leaping figure in the treble recur from time to time. Most of the characters are not given personal themes, but a jaunty march is associated with the captain, and Tausendmark has a distinctive theme which suggests stealth and a little cunning (see pp. 116-17). The opening figure of the song Jíra sings in the second scene (a) becomes an essential part of the orchestral texture at a much slower speed when he, Junoš and the chorus of peasants sing their beautiful nocturne towards the end of the opera (b) (see illustration on page 92).

It is easy to see that the Swedish symphonic poems helped Smetana to convey a series of different dramatic situations in musical terms, but naturally the opportunities in this opera were far greater. Ludiše is presented in a whole series of very varied situations, ranging from over-sweet femininity expressed in chromatic, quasi-Wagnerian terms, the direct love she has for Junoš, her angry and powerful repulse to

(a) [Allegro con fuoco]

(b) [Andantino, ma con moto]

Strings

Chorus

pp

Night is so peace - ful,___ it is so

pp

still! All is fast a - sleep,

Tausendmark's advances ('I would rather be buried in the ground than give you my hand'), her fears when alone and her terror when Tausendmark seizes her. The monologue that Tausendmark sings after having been snubbed by the captain expresses three entirely different moods, and consequently it served as a preparatory exercise for Kalina's monologue in *The Secret*, but his indecision and fears, although human enough, are unlikely to gain him any sympathy. The music of Jíra and the vagabonds has links with Czech folk song, and we are never in doubt about this truant's passionate belief in the rightness of his cause. A highlight of the work is the exhilarating dance that he and the beggars take part in, which resembles a *skočná* but includes suggestion of polka rhythm in one section. The beginning of the dance is shown here:

Allegro con fuoco

Basically this still very topical opera may be seen as a plea for the rights of the underprivileged, the peasants who protest that they are not rabble but human beings. Smetana's sympathy with them is clear enough in the scene of ferment in the Prague square, the most success-ful scene in the opera, and also in their flight into the country. But the rebellious spirit changes to a broad patriotism and a respect for those in authority as soon as they show determination to act against invaders and traitors.

The earlier versions of *The Bartered Bride* followed the *Singspiel* and *opéra comique* traditions by having spoken dialogue between the musical numbers. Originally there were two acts, no scene change in the whole work, and no dances. For the performance on 29th January 1869 Smetana divided the first act and wrote a new drinking chorus to open the second scene. He also composed a polka to precede Vašek's aria at the beginning of the second act and wrote 'That dream of love' for Mařenka. He rearranged the work in three acts for the performance on 1st June that year, adding the *furiant* to complete Act I. This resulted in Vašek's stuttering song and his duet with Mařenka being postponed until after the drinking chorus at the beginning of Act II. The couplet for the manager and Esmerelda was dropped, and the comedians' march and *skočná* (Dance of the Comedians) were added. The spoken dialogue was replaced by recitative for the new production on 25th September 1870, which changed the character of the opera radically.

The first libretto which Sabina wrote for *The Bartered Bride* was in one act, which was unacceptable to Smetana, so the librettist redrafted it in two acts, without having the slightest idea how large the opera would eventually become. Smetana was so enthusiastic about the new project that he wrote the brilliant overture before receiving the new draft, a step for which there must be few precedents in the history of opera. In his sketchbook we find sixteen bars of the opening chorus noted down with the comment 'Chorus of a comedy' as early as October 1862, and a sketch for the love duet with its lilting sixths dated 14th May 1863; yet Smetana did not receive his libretto until 5th July that year. His borrowings from *Wedding Scenes* are referred to on p. 59. According to Srb-Debrnov [1] most of the charming tunes occurred to Smetana at twilight as he walked beside the Vltava reading Sabina's libretto. He would then return to his flat to write them down. He stated in his diary (23rd April 1864) that he tried to give his opera a wholly national character because the subject demanded this.[2]

To write an operetta that has a comic marriage broker and a potential bridegroom who stutters as principal characters, and a plot centred upon a young man's trick of selling his bride to himself, was a brilliant notion. The real title of this work, 'The Sold Bride', was decided by Smetana, taking hints from A. Wehl and Jan Neruda.[3] He achieved a gaiety akin to that of his beloved Mozart, but he appears to owe more to *The Barber of Seville* than to *Figaro*,

[1] *Dalibor*, vol. 24; Bartoš, *op. cit.*

[2] A photograph of Smetana's first draft of Mařenka's accompanied recitative in Act III appears on the plate following. The whole of the pencil sketch for this work is published in facsimile (Prague, 1944). For a full discussion of this draft, see G. Abraham's 'The Genesis of The Bartered Bride' in *Slavonic and Romantic Music*.

[3] Wehl wrote 'The Bridegroom gives away his Bride', and Neruda wrote 'Sold Love'. *The Shorter Oxford Dictionary* states that 'barter' can mean 'to dispose of for a consideration, usually an unworthy one'.

SKETCH OF MAŘENKA'S 'AH! BITTERNESS! WHEN HEARTS
HAVE TRUSTED VAINLY!'
From *The Bartered Bride*

SCENES BY J. VILÍMEK FROM 'THE BARTERED BRIDE'
In *Divadelní listy*, 1882

and he undoubtedly took some hints from Van Bett's aria 'O sancto justitia!' in Lortzing's *Zar und Zimmerman* when creating the musical personality of Kecal, who is one of the best loved comic figures in opera. The pair of lovers is seen in a variety of moods and situations, which are exceptionally well suggested when their misunderstanding is at its height. Vašek's immaturity and naïvity are never in doubt for a moment. Even some of the minor characters are so well portrayed that František Bartoš has said: 'Smetana has put on the stage a slice of real life, realistically seen.'

Smetana is extremely sparing with musical cross-references, but when they occur they make their point immediately in the most natural way. When Mařenka hears that Jeník has sold her for three hundred gulden there is a quiet reminder of their love duet, and a little later when they are at cross-purposes they sing another duet during which a theme from the marriage contract music (and therefore also from the overture) enters haltingly.

Except in the *furiant*, which borrows several bars from 'Sedlák, sedlák', Smetana avoided using folk material in this opera, although from time to time there are glimpses of basic elements of Czech folk-song. Smetana's nationalism goes much deeper than this. We cannot help recognizing that the two terzettos convey two quite distinct aspects of Czech style, but if we ask ourselves why they are Czech it is not easy to give a straightforward answer. The composer certainly felt the pulse of the peasantry of his country and knew how to express this in his music, yet inevitably he added something of himself. Although *The Bartered Bride* is accepted everywhere as pure Czech music, it would be prudent to qualify this by saying that the distilla-tion of Smetana's style in this work has given us what is generally regarded as an example of pure Czech art. It embraces joy, optimism, comedy and pathos, but these are only a small part of what Smetana conceived as the spirit of his nation. His mission was incomplete until he gave an adequate musical representation of the burdens and sorrows of the Czechs, the nobility, heroism and self-sacrifice of their greatest leaders, the pride of the nation in the inherent greatness of its finest sons and their unshakable faith in the glorious future that lay ahead. Until he wrote *Dalibor* and *Libuše* he made no attempt at the musical realization, in the fullest and most comprehensive sense, of the ethos of his people.

Since the critics swayed public opinion against *Dalibor* when it was first mounted, and it failed to win support when attempts were made to revive it during the composer's lifetime, it is worth while seeing whether the critics were justified in claiming that the opera is Wagnerian, that Smetana wished to out-do *Tristan* and began at the point where Wagner left off. It is certainly true that Smetana wrote in a declamatory style at some points of the drama. There is at least one passage of chromatic polyphony that reminds us that he admired the work of Wagner, and some chromatic harmony that points in the direction of Wagner and Liszt. But there is also a great deal of diatonic writing, there are long stretches of tonic harmony, or tonic and domin-ant harmony, some borrowing from grand opera, and in the partisans' scene and even during Dalibor's trial (when he sings 'Ničím je si život'—Life is worthless to me), there are obvious echoes of Czech folk-song. This cannot be described as full-blooded Wagnerism.[1]

Transformation of theme is an important factor in *Dalibor*, just as it was in *Wallenstein's Camp*. One basic theme which was first sketched on 13th May 1863, long before Smetana started to write the opera, appears in many forms and always in association with the knight Dalibor. In the trial scene at the beginning of the work it appears first as a funeral march, modulating progressively from G minor to E flat minor, B minor and F sharp minor (see (a) page 97).[2] While Milad anxiously awaits the arrival of Dalibor, whom she has just accused of murdering her brother, the Burgrave of Ploškovice, and burning his castle, it appears at a rapid speed as shown in (b). Presently when Dalibor enters, looking every inch a hero, it is presented majestically in F sharp major (c). The same theme also represents Dalibor's greatest friend Zdeněk (d), who was foully killed by the Burgrave, and in yet another form it is associated with the attempt of Milada and the partisans to liberate Dalibor from the dungeon where he has been condemned to slow starvation (e):

[1] Smetana's attitude to Wagner is discussed on pp. 39 and 100.
[2] In the sketch the modulations are similar, but go from C minor to B minor.

Since this theme serves as the focal point of the entire opera *Dalibor* is sometimes misleadingly referred to as a monothematic work. It must not be overlooked, however, that the work also makes use of other recurring themes which have no direct connection with the Dalibor motif. One of these (quoted on p. 120) was sketched even earlier, on 28th December 1862, and very possibly symbolizes the supreme authority of King Vladislav. An ostinato bass figure is also closely associated with the King (an extract appears on p. 120). A theme sketched on 17th June 1863 is linked with Milada and also with her brother. We seem to recognize the basic element of this, a falling diminished fourth, and other features in a series of transformations, all of which are associated with Dalibor's crime of vengeance, and include his imprisonment and sentence of death.[1] Smetana still tended to conceive his work sectionally or in grouped sections, even though the music does not halt when there are scene changes within an act. Consequently there is still a relationship with the methods he used in his symphonic poems. Representative themes are used singly as motivic material or make brief appearances to make dramatic points, but are not combined to form the continuous symphonic texture that is so characteristic of the mature Wagner, whose method of climax building was therefore entirely foreign to the Czech composer's style.

Wenzig's libretto is based on the legend of a knight who rebelled against authority during the fifteenth century and was prepared to die in the cause of justice and truth. It was more than Dalibor could bear when the head of his boon companion Zdeněk was impaled on a stake, and he resolved to seek full retribution for this insult. He warns the King that he will strike more blows if he can to repay the Burgrave's crime, which forces the monarch to cast him into prison. Directly Dalibor appears before the judges Milada is astonished by his heroic bearing. She becomes ashamed of her brother's deed and regrets having brought her accusation against so noble a man, but the King makes no response when she pleads for mercy. Her love for Dalibor impels her to gain access to his cell in disguise, ostensibly to give him a violin in remembrance of Zdeněk, but in reality to give him a file and inform him of the plan for his escape.

This was the most dramatic libretto that Smetana ever used. The sudden conversion of Milada had to be made credible and was a challenge to him, and he achieved this by emphasizing the noble, frank and dauntless qualities of the hero and by making Milada respond sensitively to these and with passionate sincerity and faith try to give back to him the freedom which through her intervention he had lost. He succeeded in creating in Dalibor a character in the

[1] The sketch was used literally for the Più mosso in Act I, scene iii (full score pp. 64–6).

round and only when the hero's thoughts turn towards his dead friend and Smetana's music becomes mawkish does he disappoint. The love duet in the same scene is both tender and thrillingly optimistic. Among the lesser characters the King and the innocent and honest jailor Beneš stand out from the rest, but perhaps the crowd is handled with even greater realism and skill.

As soon as the plan to escape is uncovered Dalibor's execution is ordered. Realizing that something has gone amiss, Milada gives the signal to attack, but we are not told how it is that, in the revised ending, Dalibor succeeds in seeing Milada just after she has been mortally wounded. But at least it was advisable to bring these two together just before the final curtain. As Milada and then Dalibor die, the Dalibor theme is heard in major keys as a final catharsis in Smetana's only tragic opera.

Dalibor, as František Bartoš has pointed out, is 'concerned only with the interplay of great and positive human virtues—the redress of wrongs, faithfulness, friendship, fearlessness and courage, loyalty and self-sacrifice, and a burning, uncompromising love of freedom'. At the same time it remains within the conventions of nineteenth-century heroic opera. Smetana's extremely ambitious and grandiose fourth opera, *Libuše*, on the other hand, is in one important respect entirely without precedent in the history of opera. It was conceived as a glowing apotheosis of the greatness of the Czech nation, and herein lies its uniqueness. A work of this kind could not become a repertory opera, but would have to be reserved for performance on great national occasions. Since Franz Josef was never crowned King of Bohemia it remained unperformed until the National Theatre was opened in Prague, three years before Smetana's death. Smetana wished to present as broad a view as possible of the spirit of his nation and to give a conspectus of the country's greatness during the march of history. He therefore concentrated upon the legendary founding of the first Czech dynasty and concluded with Libuše's inspired prophesies. When Smetana had completed his opera he did not feel able to rest until he had created another great work that would be complementary to it, the cycle of symphonic poems, *My Fatherland*.

Even though *Libuše* conveys an overall sense of monumentality, an impression that grows as the work moves towards its culmination, there still remains much that we might expect to find in a more traditional work. The quarrel of the two brothers, Chrudoš and Šťáhlav, over their inheritance; the agony of Krasava, who by feign, ing love for the younger brother in order to gain the affection of the elder, drives the wedge deeper between them; Lutobor's failure to understand his daughter's dilemma—situations such as these gave Smetana the chance to make several convincing character studies, and the contrast between the impetuosity and aggressive unreason of Chrudoš and the quiet calm and fairness of Šťáhlav appealed strongly to him.

Smetana relied heavily upon a declamatory vocal style in many places, but frequently he reverted to the lyricism that is never far away in his music. It was tempting for him to move in the direction of Wagner in the more impassioned scenes, as for example when Chrudoš reacts with such violence to the judgment on the division of the inheritance, but there is no slavish imitation of the older com, poser's style, and almost invarial ly at these moments Smetana intro, duces features that are strikingly personal. He was well aware of the problem facing him and knew exactly where he stood. In writing to Adolf Čech on 4th December 1882 he said: [1]

> I am not counterfeiting [the work of] an esteemed composer; I just marvel at his greatness and make use of all that I recognize as good and beautiful and above all truthful in art. You already knew that about me long ago, but others do not know it and think I introduce Wagnerism!!! I am sufficiently occupied with Smetanism, since that is the only honest style!—for me the libretto decides the musical style.

Princess Libuše resolves to take a husband after Chrudoš has insulted her by rejecting the judgment of a court ruled by a woman, and thus the brothers' quarrel becomes a vital element in the dramatic scheme. The librettist followed the old legend closely on this point. Libuše chooses as her consort Přemysl of Stadice, to whom she has often turned for advice.

[1] P. Pražák, *Smetanovy zpěvohry*, vol. ii (Prague, 1948), p. 133.

In this opera Smetana made considerable use of sustained static harmony, just as Monteverdi did at the beginning of *Orfeo*; but whereas the Italian aroused an anticipatory excitement with his Toccata, Smetana's fanfares adopt a stately tempo in order to provide an appropriate atmosphere for his more solemn scenes. In a very different context, in the ensemble for Libuše, her minister Radovan, the thanes, jury and people at the climax of the first act, twenty-four bars of virtually pure tonic harmony are followed soon afterwards by a dominant pedal that lasts for thirty-six bars. Smetana relied on the cumulative effect that repetition of a single chord can have.

The music of Libuše and Přemysl is basically diatonic. He is serene and dignified, whereas she occasionally allows her emotions to get the upper hand. Her distress when insulted is convincing, and a refreshingly youthful excitement becomes apparent while she waits at the Vyšehrad for Přemysl's arrival. He is favoured with two of the finest parts of the opera, the splendidly sensitive and noble aria 'The sun blazes already' (Již plane slunce) and the delightfully evocative aria 'So I remain' (Já ale zůstanu) in which, while enjoying the shade of the limes, he imagines he hears the breeze whispering to him about Libuše. The harvest celebration that separates these two arias is a greatly expanded reworking for orchestra and chorus of a few bars from an album leaf in G major composed many years earlier. Smetana also borrowed from another piano work of that time, the piece *To Robert Schumann* (a), and the earlier setting of *Czech Song*, for the motif associated with Přemysl's love (b):

(*a*)   Allegro con moto

Přemysl does not appear until the second act, but his main motif is heard much earlier when Lutobor refers to him in secret conversation with Radovan. Libuše's motif is suggested near the beginning of the opera, but the complete melody is reserved for the moment when she departs in preparation for the trial. Both themes are prominent in the Prelude. When Libuše and Přemysl enter in state in the final scene their motifs become united. Chrudoš and Šťáhlav have distinctive personal themes and there is a third motif that they share. As we would expect, their themes are combined when they become reconciled. Once again, as in *Dalibor*, all these themes represent a small yet significant part of the music that the composer wrote for his characters.

FIRST PAGE OF THE SCORE OF 'FROM BOHEMIA'S FIELDS AND
FORESTS'

When the nuptials are over and Chrudoš has made an abject apology, Libuše in her ecstasy has visions of Břetislav and Jitka, Jaroslav of Šternberk, Otakar II, Eliška and Charles IV, Žižka, Prokop the Great and the Hussites, George of Poděbrady, and finally the royal castle of Prague. The fourth tableau is dominated by the Hussite chorale (see p. 83), and the powerful rhythm of this persists until the curtain falls. Libuše concludes with the words that every Czech knows by heart: 'My beloved Czech nation will not perish; gloriously she will vanquish the terrors of Hell!'

Smetana's cautious leanings towards Wagnerian style were undoubtedly a help to him with characterization, which reaches a high level in this work. He was also more successful in fusing the separate sections together. Yet there remains a certain incongruity in the opera as a whole because the range of style is rather extreme. The idyllic opening of the scene at Stadice is delightful, yet it is difficult to imagine young peasants being elated in this particular fashion. Smetana also seems to have miscalculated a little in placing quite so much reliance on simple tonic and dominant harmony when aiming at an exalted monumental style. It is refreshing when, as happens frequently, he breaks away from diatonicism with unexpected chromaticism and modulations to unrelated keys. When *Libuše* is viewed dispassionately its many virtues are seen to outweigh any shortcomings, and it will be recognized as a splendid achievement.

CHAPTER XIII

OPERA (2)

THE LYRICAL AND ROMANTIC WORKS

Turning from the national operas to those that followed is like entering another world, but the gulf is greatest of all between *Libuše* and Smetana's next work for the stage, *The Two Widows*. It is easy to see how he relished this opportunity to relax and unbend in the wake of his great festival work, but with *The Bartered Bride* as a precedent for comic opera it is surprising to find him writing a frivolous and intimate conversation piece for a very small cast and choosing a country estate as the setting. In the first version there were only four characters. The vivacious and coquettish Caroline serves as a foil for her cousin Agnes, who is troubled because during her husband's lifetime she admired Ladislav, a well-to-do young landowner. She has felt it her duty to continue wearing mourning during her two years of widowhood. Ladislav pretends to poach on Caroline's land so as to meet Agnes again, and so the suspicious and scheming Caroline orders her thick-headed gamekeeper Mumlal[1] to arrest him. There was no aria for Ladislav, who had to be content with a hundred bars of solo during the mock trial (a quartet). This version included spoken dialogue. Three years later Smetana added two minor characters, peasant lovers, who appear in the newly composed finale to the first act, and in a trio with Mumlal. He also gave a solo song to Ladislav and set the dialogue in recitative. After the Hamburg performance Smetana composed a new trio for the first act and revised the ending of Agnes's big aria, but the orchestral versions of these are now missing.

The composer was so captivated by the possibilities of his new work that he seems to have temporarily forgotten the trouble he had

---

[1] The Czech verb 'mumlat' means to mumble.

been having with the critics. The slender, artificial and farcical libretto fired his imagination, and making use of four sketches which originated from seven to ten years earlier and working rapidly he produced this sparkling work. Plasticity seemed essential to him, and so he changed the style of his recitative frequently and interrupted his arias and ensembles with recitative passages. This made sudden changes of mood easier and gave opportunities to convey the finer points of characterization, and in consequence the whole work possesses a flexibility without parallel before the time of Richard Strauss. Strauss was particularly fond of *The Two Widows* and perhaps came closest to its style in his *Intermezzo*.

Formal reminiscence themes would have been out of place in this opera, but there are themes associated with Ladislav and Agnes, and the 'bull in a china shop' motif that accompanies Mumlal's first entry is referred to again later. Ladislav's love theme is heard when he begins to quote from his letter to Agnes during their duet, and later in the same number he recites the remainder of the letter (i.e. melodrama) against a musical background formed almost entirely out of this melodic phrase. The same theme is briefly recalled when Agnes in her anguish remembers him saying that he wished to give his whole heart to her alone, and when Ladislav confesses to Caroline that it was love that drove him to her mansion. Smetana found just what he wanted to represent Agnes's feelings of guilt in an eighteen-bar sketch which he made ten years earlier, on 5th June 1863. At that early date it was fully worked out with an accompaniment, and it needed little alteration for inclusion at the beginning of the quartet where, accompanied by solo cello and horn, she sings 'Oh! how anxious I feel about meeting him here.' It is hinted at in her duet with Caroline and again prominent at the beginning of the melodrama-duet when she takes out Ladislav's letter, then decides to destroy it, but burns only a little of it and reads it again. In the trio in recitative, while Caroline encourages the woebegone widow to bury herself alive and Ladislav urges the exact opposite, the same theme is ironically transmuted into a slow waltz. When Ladislav tells Caroline he was enchanted by her ball there is a further reference to the waltz, which informs us that while he danced with Caroline he was confident of winning Agnes.

The ensembles and recitatives give us a more complete picture of Caroline than is possible in her aria, which again stems from a sketch made in 1863. The fine *scena* for Agnes, on the other hand, tells us a great deal about her anguish and conscience-stricken state of mind. The relentless nature of her torment is vividly conveyed in one section by a most persistent throbbing rhythmic ostinato of triplets and semi-quavers for the horns. She is much the most interesting character in this polished and light-hearted work. Richard Gorer has drawn attention [1] to the orchestra's 'polite commonplaces' which give added poignancy to the impassioned phrases of Agnes and Ladislav in the middle of their duet, and cites this as the kind of thing Smetana meant when he spoke of this opera's 'distinguished salon style'. Finally, mention must be made of the splendid polka which enriches the end of the work.

Like *The Bartered Bride*, Smetana's next two operas, *The Kiss* and *The Secret*, are based on life in the countryside, but they have few other points of resemblance with the earlier work. *The Kiss* was Smetana's first opera to be composed after he was afflicted by total deafness, a fact that affected the style of the new work. On the whole it is a cheerful opera and it even contains farcical elements, notably in the scene in which Vendulka and her smuggler aunt, Martinka, encounter a frontier guard, but it is not frivolous like *The Two Widows*. It is more intimate and subjective than any of the previous operas, and consequently we learn much more about the psychology of Vendulka and Lukaš than of the earlier quarrelling lovers, Mařenka and Jeník. The plot of the opera is extremely slender, centring as it does on a trivial point of etiquette—Vendulka's refusal to allow her widower bridegroom-to-be to kiss her, because she is determined to do nothing that might disturb the repose of the deceased woman before Lukaš and she are formally married. But at least it gave Smetana the chance to present his hero and heroine as credible human beings, and to con-trast them with the vivacious, optimistic and self-confident Martinka, the apprehensive and gloomy father of the bride, the match-maker Tomeš, who by his persistence triumphs in difficult circumstances,

[1] 'Smetana's Conversation Opera', in *The Listener*, 14th October 1965.

the kindly and sympathetic smuggler Matouš, who plays a key part towards the final reconciliation, and finally the delightfully effusive young maid Barče. Furthermore, the composer was strongly attracted by the eerie nocturnal atmosphere of the forest scene in which the smugglers appear, and he sketched the smugglers' chorus first of all.[1]

Since Act I and the two scenes of Act II are broadly conceived as complete entities and there is a strong emphasis on lyricism, *The Kiss* has in certain respects a closer affinity with *Dalibor* and *Libuše* than with *The Two Widows*. The most conspicuous recurring theme is the one in polka rhythm associated with the shameful roistering behaviour of Lukaš, who gets drunk and returns with the village girls to taunt Vendulka. It is a variant on the revelry theme in *Šárka*. Although rarely heard, next in importance comes the theme symbolizing the joyful prospect for Lukaš of being united at last with the girl he loved before his parents forced him to marry another, a theme of reunification rather than of reconciliation. It is announced immediately the marriage is agreed to, and has already been heard at the beginning of the over-ture. A significant third motif is heard when Tomeš persuades Lukaš that he must apologize publicly, and Martinka has a personal theme which appears towards the end of the first act. It is puzzling why the first bar of the smugglers' march should be worked into the previous act at the point where Lukaš is brought by the match-maker to the home of his future bride.

Martinka's comic rôle is conceived with much greater subtlety than that of the father, and she is shown in a particularly attractive light when she throws out hints that Vendulka might consider joining the smugglers. While confusion reigns during the trio for these two and the frontier guard, the orchestra plays a delightful dance. The violently contrasting moods of Lukaš are conveyed particularly well, which makes him one of the most convincing characters in Smetana's operas. The lyrical beauty of Vendulka's music is especially memorable, and reaches its highest level in her song when Lukaš's baby is brought in, when she is so distressed after his departure in a towering rage, and

[1] A few bars of the music for Tomeš when he appears in the forest were sketched nine years earlier in October 1866.

when she sings the second of the two lullabies.[1] The transition from this lullaby to the rowdy return of Lukaš provides an excellent example of Smetana's skill in handling a dramatic contrast. The work as a whole has a simplicity, a naturalness and dramatic fitness, coupled with the 'peculiar sentimental glow', as František Bartoš describes it, of its lyrical sections. But we can also sense a growing spirit of optimism, which is due to the composer's discovery that he possessed the power to overcome his tragic physical disability.

Smetana's next opera, *The Secret*, is an attractive blend of serious, romantic and comic elements, merged with touches of fantasy, and is given an eighteenth-century setting. The feud between the two town councillors, Kalina and Malina, unlike that between Montague and Capulet, is rooted in a disparity of wealth, but as in Shakespeare their son and daughter, Vít and Blaženka, are secretly in love. Kalina is embittered because his poverty alone prevented him from marrying Malina's sister Roza. She is firmly convinced that Kalina, now a widower, was untrue to her when he married another, because the deceased Friar Barnabáš told her that he had given Kalina secret information about how he could win her. She has remained single. Kalina has no knowledge of these instructions, but when the old veteran Bonifác, who is himself attempting to court Roza, finds a dilapidated piece of paper in a crevice, Kalina recognizes that this is from the friar, and learns from it that there is treasure to be found beneath the ruins of Bezděz castle.

There was more scope for a composer with a genuine stage sense in a plot having this situation as its starting point than there was in *The Kiss*. Smetana had written for hostile crowds before, but not for two similar factions who are provoked so much that they come to blows. The conflicts and tensions between the principal characters—Kalina, Malina, Roza and Bonifác—were a vital stimulus to him. The clandestine meetings of the youthful lovers, their dreams and their disappointments, provided a series of refreshing interludes and quite exceptional opportunities for lyricism and sentiment. Even minor characters have a vital rôle to play. Skřivánek, the ballad singer, attempts the impossible when trying to sing a song that will satisfy Kalina and Malina,

[1] Smetana used the folk-song 'Andulka, mé dítě' for the first lullaby.

and which in fact infuriates both of them and upsets Roza and Bonifác as well. The master builder plays a less significant part, but his concern about receiving payment for Kalina's fine new house prompts Bonifác to disclose in the strictest confidence that, thanks to Friar Barnabáš, Kalina is expecting to find treasure. However, tongues will wag, and within minutes the news is proclaimed through a megaphone from the church tower.

But it is Kalina who very rightly attracts most of our attention and sympathy. For twenty years he proudly tried to live down his bitter disappointment over Roza, and by pinching and scraping strove unceasingly to become prosperous. His enemy Malina knows full well that the new house is merely a façade to conceal his plight. The message of Barnabáš kindles fresh hope, and with it a feverish craving for riches, which Kalina vaguely links with Roza. While he sleeps the ghost of the friar appears to him, speaking somewhat enigmatically, but there are also evil spirits dancing around, who make him aware that he may be selling his soul to the devil for mammon. His dilemma is intensified by the presence of church-goers, whom he decides to join. But in the end he feels compelled to dig for the treasure, whatever the risk and despite Roza's attempted intervention, and so he vanishes underground. In the second act of *The Secret* Kalina stands out as one of Smetana's finest characterizations.

In a letter to Adolf Čech Smetana said:[1] 'There are two main motifs: the motif on "the secret" (treasure), and of Kalina, out of which as it were the whole edifice of the opera is constructed and from which other subordinate motifs are derived, although indepen- dent individual singing occurs, especially songs of national style, etc.' It is certainly true that the motif of the secret is of paramount importance. Scored for trombones, horns, timpani and tremolando strings, it is the most striking of all Smetana's operatic motifs, and in its own way has a similar significance to Samiel's motif in *Der Freischütz*. However, it is misleading to couple it with Kalina's motif, for this is not particularly distinctive and is seldom employed. There are remarkably few motifs in this opera, but a third might be

[1] 4th September 1878; Pražák, *Smetanovy zpěvohry*, vol. iii, p. 252.

mentioned: the one associated with the solemn but farcical promise to keep the secret. Even though the main motif occurs with great effect in one form or another in a score of places, we would be wrong to describe *The Secret* as monothematic, but the overture most certainly is.[1]

In its principal and rather ominous form the motif of the secret treasure is heard for the first time in the opera when Roza mentions Barnabáš to Bonifác, and explains why she believes that Kalina betrayed her (a). The theme lends itself very readily to imitations and sequential treatment in diminution. The dance of the gnomes is accompanied by a particularly deft and attractive fugal transformation of the same theme (b), which is entirely different from the serious fugue on the same basic theme in the overture. At the denouement, when Kalina has overcome his bewilderment at emerging from the tunnel into Malina's house, has discovered that Roza is the treasure he sought, and has asked Malina to allow his son Vít to marry Blaženka, the same theme takes on a new form that accurately reflects the general atmosphere of rejoicing (c):

(a) Largo

(b) Allegro vivo

[1] Apart from slight references to the music of the elves and gnomes, the entire overture is based on the 'secret' motif.

(c) [Più allegro]

With so much genuine drama Smetana felt it necessary to resort frequently to recitative, while retaining an unbroken line of musico-dramatic thought. We frequently notice that when a vocal line is fragmented the stream of orchestral sound continues unabated. The richness of the writing for treble strings and woodwind is most impressive and seems to reach a peak in this work. In one case Smetana deliberately introduced a closed form—the sad song that Blaženka sings in the last act—but the ballad singer's contribution is entirely different and is fully integrated into the surrounding music. Kalina and Malina interrupt him in recitative after the second verse. During the third verse there are electrifying interjections from Roza, Bonifác, Malina and the chorus, and the orchestral temperature rises rapidly. Then while the hubbub continues and the music pursues its headlong course, the second half of the stanza is completed by the obstinate singer. Without question *The Secret* has a great deal to offer to audiences outside Czechoslovakia, and deserves to be far better known.

Smetana always made certain that each new opera would be different from those he had composed previously. When he came to the last of the series, *The Devil's Wall*, he subtitled it 'comic-romantic opera', a description that would also have fitted *The Secret*,[1] According to an old legend the devil attempted to divert the river

[1] Smetana almost certainly considered the thirteenth-century setting of *The Devil's Wall* to be more 'romantic' than the eighteenth-century. *The Secret* is subtitled 'comic opera'.

Vltava by creating a towering wall of rock near Vyšší Brod, in order to prevent a monastery from being founded there, but he was defeated by spiritual powers. In the opera the hermit Beneš covets the position of abbot for himself, and plans to secure for the monastery the riches of Lord Vok of Rožmberk, Chief Marshal of Bohemia. In conse-quence of this he puts himself completely in the power of the Prince of Darkness, Rarach, and so becomes an embodiment of the devil. Before destroying the monastery Rarach schemes to frustrate Vok's hope of marriage and to force him instead to espouse the church.

It is difficult to be sure of the precise extent of Rarach's responsibility for the sequence of events, but up to a point he manipulates matters to suit himself. He does not appear to have influenced the widowed Countess of Šauenburk to reject Vok's suit, nor to cause his envoy, the loyal and devoted knight Jarek, to swear that he himself will not marry Katuška until Vok has found a bride, but the devil turns both of these events to his advantage. The virtual identity of Beneš and Rarach is suggested visually when the latter appears as the double of Beneš. When they are both on the stage together Beneš vainly struggles against the evil power. Vok, however, sees only one of them at a time and assumes this to be his trusted spiritual adviser. At other times if only one of them is present, there may be some doubt as to which this is unless the Rarach theme or diabolical laughter are heard. In the second and third acts Rarach adopts the alternative disguise of a shepherd. Only occasionally, when the sign of the cross has been made, does he revert to his normal demonic form.

Smetana was half inclined to regard the part of Beneš as a comic rôle, 'but for the fact that he sings with Vok and the devil in serious numbers'.[1] Rarach is no comic devil of the Czech fairy tales, but has a caustic and sarcastic wit. Michálek, Vok's elderly steward, who has hopes that his daughter Katuška will marry Vok instead of Jarek, which would make him the marshal's father-in-law, is the chief comic character and a buffo tenor. When Beneš needs to make a full con-fession of his sins but has no ordained priest to turn to, the only

[1] Letter to Adolf Čech, 4th June 1882; Pražák, *Smetanovy zpěvohry*, vol. iv, pp. 73–5.

person available for this purpose is Michálek. Curiously enough, in this farcical scene he rids himself of Rarach's power by means of this perverse action.

The Devil's Wall has more than the normal number of reminiscence themes, but only four of these have particular significance. Vok is given a march-like theme that recalls some of the pageantry of Libuše. Hedvika, the Countess's daughter, who becomes Vok's ward on her mother's death and ultimately becomes his bride, is represented by a gracefully curling theme in thirds. Yet another theme is invariably associated with Jarek's oath[1] and finally there is Rarach's highly characteristic motif based on a progression of augmented triads (a). The satanic spirit of this theme has its antithesis in the enchanting pastoral mood of the second theme quoted here (b):

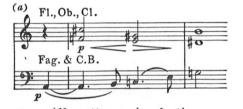

This too is an accurate musical representation of Rarach—but of Rarach acting the part of a shepherd to perfection. Later when his flock is changed into a host of demons, this innocent theme becomes transformed into a diabolical dance.

There are surprisingly few signs in this work that Smetana's powers

[1] This theme was sketched during October 1875, before Smetana received the libretto of *The Kiss*.

were diminishing, even though composition was such a labour to him and the work of creation was so protracted. His musical imagination was as lively as ever and his command of chromatic harmony and enharmonic modulation remained strong. However, he and his librettist appear to have agreed upon a rather feeble means of relieving the tension after Beneš has driven Rarach away and before the devil returns in a tempest to build his wall. Since Smetana's opera has occasional pointers towards his second String Quartet, that somewhat problematical work would be better understood if approached by way of *The Devil's Wall*.

The charming duet for Katuška and Jarek, which is so characteristic of the composer, the glowing description that Záviš[1] gives of Hedvika to his Uncle Vok, and the splendidly impressive utterance of Hedvika on her arrival, are among the most memorable parts of the opera. Smetana, however, had the highest regard for Vok's 'Jen jediná mě ženy krásné tvář', from the first act. During this aria Vok recalls the joy of his love for the beautiful Countess of Šauenburk in the springtime of his life. But since she refused him, and died soon afterwards, he is haunted by her image and only bitter memories remain. Smetana told his librettist[2] that he was invariably carried away when he sang this song to himself, and he added: 'It always moves me to tears, for it sprang from the heart and almost describes my unhappy state.'

Smetana wrote *The Devil's Wall* with the intention of creating a comic opera embodying various elements of parody. The parodies of representatives of the church, in the form of mock liturgical chanting, a comic conferring of absolution after confession, and spiritual advice given and worldly rewards sought by a hypocrite with a dual personality—these are abundantly clear. To these is added the portrait of a sycophantic steward. Očadlík has pointed out[3] that in a broader sense the composer also hoped to create a kind of parody of a drama of romantic chivalry, employing the customary oaths, evasions

[1] A travesty part for a contralto.

[2] Letter of 16th February 1880; Očadlík, *Eliška Krásnohorská—Bedřich Smetana*, pp. 161–3.

[3] Handbook to the Supraphon gramophone records.

and intrigues, and he also observed that Vok, who cannot find a bride, is a comic-opera equivalent of the Flying Dutchman. Since the libretto was over-long, Smetana was expected to cut it and he did so by omitting some of the comic episodes. By doing this, and also thanks to his inclination to identify in some measure his hero with himself, the primary aim of the opera became modified. In certain respects this last opera of Smetana's, which is such an interesting blend of national choruses, powerful dramatic scenes, a considerable amount of parodistic comedy and a great deal of lyricism, still remains something of an enigma. But this gives it an added fascination.

CHAPTER XIV

CHARACTERISTICS OF SMETANA'S STYLE
AND HIS ACHIEVEMENT

Even the most nationally minded composer, particularly if he is the first of a line, can hardly avoid seeing what he can learn from the example of his contemporaries and forerunners in other countries. This is certainly true of Smetana who, as we have already noticed, was keenly alive to the more progressive musical developments of his time, and was influenced strongly by Schumann, Berlioz, Wagner and above all by Liszt. The indigenous musical influence that affected him most strongly undoubtedly came from Czech folk-song and dance. Polka rhythms are quite often encountered in his music when he was not writing a formal dance, but the characteristic *furiant* cross-rhythm which Dvořák favoured is extremely rare in Smetana's compositions. Cross-rhythms in fact are not often found except as quavers combined with triplets (two against three). A splendid example of this may be seen in the finale of his Piano Trio. In Czech folk-song the initial figure of the first phrase is sometimes repeated, as in 'Má milá, má milá, černé oči máte' (a).[1] Occasionally Smetana did the same thing, as for instance in the introductory bars to Mařenka's duet with Jeník, in the trio in Act I of *The Bartered Bride* and also in Tausendmark's motif in *The Brandenburgers in Bohemia* (b):

(a)

[1] Other examples include 'Hrály dudy', 'Já mám koně, vrany koně', 'Kdyby moje milá', 'Ovčáci!', 'Strejček Nimra' and 'Za háj'.

čím je u - mej - vá - te?

(b) Moderato

Strings *p*
p pizz.

The 'Three Blind Mice' figure in the last bar of this folk-song can also be traced in the opera choruses and in Blaženka's lament in *The Secret*, but neither of these devices occurs nearly as often as in Dvořák's music. In general Smetana came closest to the folk spirit in his choruses of peasants, where we also encounter the three-bar phrases of Czech folk-song. Although Vendulka's second lullaby is sometimes referred to as being in folk style, it possesses some features which are foreign to it. The ballad singer's song in *The Secret*, on the other hand, is a much better example of a pseudo folk-song.

Smetana could not avoid being affected by the metre of the verses he set. In the Czech language the almost unvaried stresses on first syllables [1] lead to ubiquitous trochaic rhythms. These played an even greater rôle in Dvořák's style than in that of the German-educated Smetana; but when the latter set words it became extremely common

[1] In the folk-song quoted above the rhythm on the words 'Má milá' is as faulty as if the words were 'My sweetheart'. The prosody is obsolete.

for his choral entries in particular to fall on strong beats.[1] Inevitably Smetana submitted far more readily to linguistic influences in crowd and comic scenes than he did in dramatic episodes and noble and lyrical passages.

Except in pieces of the *moto perpetuo* type and *buffo* patter songs it is not usual for composers to maintain an unbroken flow of notes of equal rhythmic value over an extended period of time. Continuous quavers or crotchets, however, appealed to Smetana, both as the main thematic interest and also as an accompaniment to rhythmically varied vocal parts, and they are not necessarily confined to comic contexts. In *Dalibor* Milada's appeal and the jury's replies are accompanied for more than seventy bars with quavers arranged as pairs of repeated notes. A similar duplication of a basic crotchet rhythm continues for well over a hundred bars, with only brief interruptions, in the duet for Ladislav and Mumlal in *The Two Widows*, and the main theme of the finale of the *Triumphal Symphony* keeps strictly to crotchet rhythm for almost seventy bars. In the six-eight finale of the Piano Trio another long passage occurs, but in this case there is a melody of repeated couplets and an accompaniment of continuous quavers.

The symphonic poem *Blaník* includes a particularly interesting passage nearly sixty bars long which is highly characteristic of the composer. A triplet rhythm is maintained, but quavers are sometimes superimposed upon this. The first six bars, quoted below, are twice repeated sequentially a fourth higher each time. The basic notes of each bar (d', d, e, a, in bar 1) are anticipated during the preceding beats, and the entire passage continues in this manner. Furthermore the first bar, which is repeated, strongly reminds us of the codetta of the *Bartered Bride* overture.

Meno mosso

[1] The influence of folk-song on Dvořák's style is discussed in Chapter II of my book *Antonín Dvořák: Musician and Craftsman* (London, 1966).

SMETANA
Posthumous charcoal drawing by Max Švabinský, of 1904

An example of chordal anticipations may be seen in the second *Poetic Polka*. The Sousedská in the *Czech Dances* includes a twelve-bar passage in quaver chords which has a three-fold repetition of the initial bar, and sequential repetition besides. Only Smetana could have written this:

In discussing *Libuše* attention was drawn to stretches of completely static harmony. Pedal basses provide stability yet offer opportunities for considerable harmonic variety, and besides the pedal note may change, as we see in a hundred-bar section of the duet for Mařenka and Vašek in *The Bartered Bride*. (The successive pedal notes are F, D flat, A, F and A flat.) One of the most persistent mannerisms in Smetana's music is the alternation of tonic and dominant harmony. Good instances may be seen at the point where the cradle is brought in in *The Kiss*, and in two places towards the end of *Vltava*.[1] Twenty-four bars before the end of this work the alternations occur over a tonic pedal. Both of the themes associated with King Vladislav in *Dalibor* fall into the tonic-dominant category. The one that I have suggested earlier as symbolizing his supreme authority is as perfect an example as any of this trait (a), whereas an extract from the King's basic motif shows it in a slightly elaborated form (b):

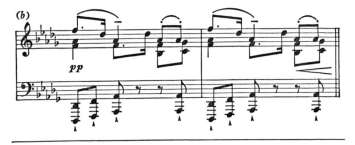

---

[1] There is a shift of tonic in a similar passage in *Wayfarer's Song*, and in the slow movement of the *Triumphal Symphony* the key changes from G sharp minor to F sharp major, followed by perfect cadences in the major keys of F, E, E flat and D.

It requires very little imagination to see that the extract quoted higher up (p. 119) from the Sousedská may be regarded as yet another example of alternating tonic and dominant chords, but one that shows even greater elaboration.

Smetana was keenly aware of the limited value of the influence of folk music on his art, and since most of his Czech predecessors wrote in styles that were similar to those of their contemporaries in other countries, he could expect little from their example to help him in his aim to write in a truly Czech manner. In approaching this subject we immediately become aware of the difficulty of distinguishing what is typically Czech and what is pure Smetana in the creative work of this composer. We may claim, for example, that the opening section of *From Bohemia's Fields and Forests* breathes the spirit of the Czech countryside. But alternatively is it not equally plausible to regard this as a musical realization of the impression that the countryside made on Smetana, and recognize what he wrote as a document that throws greater light on an aspect of his psychological make-up than it does on the object he had in mind? No two Czech composers would react to their fields and forests in precisely the same way, nor, supposing they did, would they, for technical reasons, produce similar music in such circumstances. Smetana's musical impression represents one of numerous possible artistic interpretations, and a perfectly sincere and valid one.

Although he was an easy prey to the jealousy and petty-mindedness of others, he had a keen understanding and appreciation of human character, and even in his darkest days he retained a streak of humour. Without these invaluable assets and his strong feeling for drama he would have been less distinguished as an opera composer, and unable to provide his people with so fine and broadly based an operatic repertory. Being a 'progressive' composer he paid scant attention to works in classical forms, and concentrated instead on the symphonic poem, in which he was outstanding. He enriched the literature of piano salon pieces, preferring to give these greater substance than was customary in this genre. He took very little notice of the art song, but wrote successfully for male voice choir, leaving the sphere of larger choral composition open for Dvořák. Thanks to his orientation towards the Viennese classics and his friendship with Brahms, Dvořák poured out a stream of symphonies and chamber music, areas in which Fibich also showed considerable interest. All three composers wrote operas, and Fibich wrote several melodramas in addition, but in opera Smetana was the best equipped of the three. It is remarkable and extremely fortunate that the creative work of Smetana and Dvořák is complementary. Much lip-service has been paid outside Czechoslovakia to Smetana as the musical leader of the national Czech movement, with a deplorably sketchy knowledge of the music to support this assumption. Once we become familiar with his music as a whole he emerges as a composer with a most distinctive and easily recognizable personality, one who succeeded in completing a Herculean task, and who when compared with the pygmies who preceded him gives us the impression that he was a giant.

The contrast between the state of music in Russia and Bohemia at the advent of Glinka and Smetana was sufficiently great for these two composers to earn the title of 'father' of Russian and Czech music in quite different ways. The educated Russians had relied on music imported from abroad for several decades, whereas Bohemia and Moravia, owing to their geographical position and especially their proximity to Vienna, were already deeply involved in European music. Although he was an amateur, Glinka succeeded in writing music in a mixture of styles, that was accepted as 'Russian' by composers who followed him and which they regarded as an important model. Smetana on the other hand was a professional who forged a national style which is indistinguishable from his personal style. He provided his country with a basic repertory of music that holds an esteemed position beside some of the finest masterpieces of his European contemporaries, and at the same time he crystallized the spirit of his nation in his art. Thus he is seen to be a unique figure in the history of music.

APPENDIX A

(Figures in brackets denote the age reached by the person mentioned during the year in question.)

Year	Age	Life	Contemporary Musicians

1824 — Bedřich Smetana born, 2 March, at Litomyšl, in north-east Bohemia, son of František Smetana (1777–1857), brewer to Count Waldstein, and his third wife Barbora, née Lynek (1791–1864); the eleventh child of František and his first son to survive birth.

Bruckner born, 4 Sept.; Cornelius born, 24 Dec.; Reinecke born, 23 June.

Adam aged 21; Alkan 11; Auber 42; Balfe 16; Beethoven 54; Bellini 23; Berlioz 21; Berwald 28; Boieldieu 49; Cherubini 64; Chopin 14; Clementi 72; Dargomizhsky 11; Donizetti 27; Field 42; Flotow 12; Franck 2; Franz 9; Gade 7; Glinka 19; Gossec 90; Gounod 6; Gyrowetz 61; Halévy 25; Henselt 10; Hérold 33; Hummel 46; Kalkbrenner 39; Lalo 1; Lesueur 64; Liszt 13; Loewe 28; Lortzing 23; Marschner 29; Mendelssohn 15; Mercadante 29; Meyerbeer 33; Moniuszko 4; Moscheles 30; Nicolai 14; Offenbach 5; Paer 52; Pleyel 67; Raff 2; Reicha 54; Rossini 32; Schubert 27; Schumann 14; Škroup (F.) 23; Spohr 40; Spontini 50; Thalberg 12; Thomas (A.) 13; Tomášek 50; Verdi 11; Vieuxtemps 4; Voříšek 33; Wagner 11; Weber 38.

Year	*Age*	*Life*	*Contemporary Musicians*
1825	1		Strauss (J. ii) born, 25 Oct.; Vojáček born, 4 Dec.; Voříšek (34) dies, 19 Nov.
1826	2		Weber (39) dies, 4–5 June.
1827	3		Beethoven (56) dies, 26 March.
1828	4	Receives elementary instruction in music from his father.	Schubert (31) dies, 19 Nov.
1829	5	Attends the Piarist School. Plays in string quartet.	Gossec (95) dies, 16 Feb.; Rubinstein born, 28 Nov.
1830	6	Has violin lessons from Chmelík. Appears as solo pianist at the Philosophical Academy, Litomyšl, 4 Oct.	Goldmark born, 18 May; Skuherský born, 31 July.
1831	7	Attends the primary school at Jindřichův Hradec, where his father is brewer to Count Czernin.	Pleyel (74) dies, 14 Nov.
1832	8	Has violin and piano lessons from Ikavec, and is soprano soloist in the church choir.	Clementi (80) dies, 10 March; Lecocq born, 3 June.
1833	9	Galop composed at about this time. Excellent progress at school leads to him being transferred to the grammar school.	Borodin born, 11 Nov.; Brahms born, 7 May; Hérold (41) dies, 19 Jan.; Rozkošný born, 21 Sept.
1834	10	The Smetanas are friendly with the Kolář family. Bedřich leaves school prematurely for an unknown reason.	Blodek born, 3 Oct.; Boieldieu (58) dies, 8 Oct.
1835	11	His father retires to a country estate. Bedřich is sent away to attend the grammar school at Jihlava, where he is homesick. Has violin lessons with Maťocha, but makes little progress at school.	Bellini (33) dies. 23 Sept.; Cui born, 18 Jan.; Saint-Saëns born, 9 Oct.; Wieniawski born, 10 July.
1836	12	Is sent to the grammar school at Německý Brod, but has to start in the lowest class.	Delibes born, 21 Feb.; Reicha (66) dies, 28 May.
1837	13	Often visits Father Šindelář, who is fond of music. Becomes friendly with his schoolfellow Karel Havlíček, a young poet.	Balakirev born, 2 Jan.; Field (54) dies, 11 Jan.; Hummel (58) dies, 17 Oct.; Lesueur (77) dies, 6 Oct.

Year	Age	Life	Contemporary Musicians
1838	14	Misses his friends Havlíček and Butula, who have left school and gone to Prague.	Bendl born, 16 April; Bizet born, 25 Oct.; Bruch born, 6 Jan.
1839	15	Attends the Academic Grammar School in Prague, and sees his friends again. Begins to enjoy the musical delights of Prague.	Mussorgsky born, 21 March; Paer (67) dies, 3 May.
1840	16	Plays truant from school. Composes for his friends. Hears Liszt play. His father discovers he has made no progress at school. Is sent to stay with his uncle at Pilsen in order to attend school there.	Goetz born, 7 Dec.; Svendsen born, 30 Sept.; Tchaikovsky born, 7 May.
1841	17	Being a gifted pianist, he is much sought after to play for dancing in the homes of rich families. Meets Kateřina Kolář again and is charmed by her.	Chabrier born, 18 Jan.; Dvořák born, 8 Sept.; Pedrell born 19 Feb.
1842	18	Composes an overture for piano duet for Kateřina's name-day and a *Galop Bajaderek* for large orchestra.	Boito born, 24 Feb.; Cherubini (81) dies, 15 March; Massenet born, 12 May; Sullivan born, 13 May.
1843	19	Decides to make music his career. Leaves school after matriculation. Since his father is in financial difficulties he goes to Prague with only twenty gulden. Hires a piano. Tries to see Kateřina.	Grieg born, 15 June; Šebor born, 13 Aug.
1844	20	Has lessons in Theory from Proksch. Commences duties as resident piano tutor to Count Thun's household (18 Jan.), a post he holds for three years. *Bagatelles and Impromptus* composed.	Rimsky-Korsakov born, 18 March.
1845	21	Studies with Proksch continue.	Fauré born, 12 May.
1846	22	Hears Berlioz conduct his *Symphonie fantastique* (Jan.) and *Romeo and Juliet* (March) and	

Year	Age	Life	Contemporary Musicians
		probably meets him at a soirée. Piano Sonata in G minor composed.	
1847	23	Meets Robert and Clara Schumann at Count Thun's. Ends his studies with Proksch and leaves the Thun household. Aims to establish himself as a virtuoso pianist. Is praised for his playing at a Prague chamber concert (12 Dec.).	Mendelssohn (38) dies, 4 Nov.
1848	24	Plans to open a music school and asks for aid from Liszt. Liszt accepts a dedication, but gives no financial support. Smetana helps to man barricades in the Revolution (11 June) and writes patriotic music. Music school opened 8 Aug.	Donizetti (50) dies, 8 April; Duparc born, 21 Jan.; Parry born, 27 Feb.
1849	25	Takes aristocratic pupils and visits Prague Castle to play to Ferdinand V. Marries Kateřina Kolář (27 Aug.). Composes *Album Leaves* and *Wedding Scenes*.	Chopin (39) dies, 17 Oct.; Kalkbrenner (63) dies, 10 June; Nicolai (38) dies, 11 May.
1850	26	For several years he finds it a struggle to make ends meet.	Fibich born, 21 Dec.; Gyrowetz (87) dies, 19 March; Tomášek (75) dies, 3 April.
1851	27	His first daughter Bedřiška born, 7 Jan.	d'Indy born, 27 March; Lortzing (49) dies, 21 Jan.; Spontini (76) dies, 24 Jan.;
1852	28	A second daughter, Gabriela, born, 26 Feb.	Stanford born, 30 Sept.
1853	29	His third daughter, Žofie, born, 24 May. *Triumphal Symphony* composed.	
1854	30	Gabriela dies of tuberculosis, 9 July.	Humperdinck born, 1 Sept.; Janáček born, 3 July.
1855	31	Bedřiška dies, 6 Sept. Writes Trio in G minor in memory of her. A fourth daughter, Kate-	Chausson born, 20 Jan.

Year	Age	Life	Contemporary Musicians

řina, born 25 Oct., but dies within eight months. His wife has tuberculosis.

1856 32 Depressed by the political situation and family economics. Has long conversations with Liszt (Sept.). Decides to try teaching in Göteborg, and leaves home, 11 Oct. Gives recitals, becomes conductor of a choral society and opens a music school in Göteborg.

Adam (52) dies, 3 May; Schumann (46) dies, 29 July; Sinding born, 11 Jan.; Taneyev born, 25 Nov.

1857 33 Unable to meet the great demand for piano lessons. Organizes chamber concerts, conducts *Elijah* and plays Beethoven's third Piano Concerto. Meets Fröjda Benecke, who strongly attracts him. Attends his father's funeral. Sees Liszt on his way back to Göteborg.

Elgar born, 2 June; Glinka (52) dies, 15 Feb.

1858 34 Performs Wagner choruses and other contemporary music in Göteborg. Completes his symphonic poem *Richard III* at Särö, where he has taken Kateřina for her health.

Leoncavallo born, 8 March; Puccini born, 22 Dec.

1859 35 *Wallenstein's Camp* completed January. Arranges farewell concerts and departs with his sick wife for home. Kateřina dies at Dresden (19 April). He is Liszt's guest at Weimar. Becomes engaged to Bettina Ferdinand. Returns to Sweden.

Foerster born, 30 Dec.; Spohr (75) dies, 22 Oct.

1860 36 Performs his *Triumphal Symphony* and plays Weber's Concertstück in Göteborg. At work on his third symphonic

Albéniz born, 29 May; Mahler born, 7 July; Wolf born, 13 March.

Year	Age	Life	Contemporary Musicians
		poem, *Haakon Jarl*. Watches the political situation following Solferino (1859), which may open up the possibility of becoming his nation's musical leader. Remarries (10 July) and returns to Göteborg with Bettina.	
1861	37	*Haakon Jarl* completed 24 March. Plays to royalty in Stockholm (10 April). Successful recital at Norrköping. Arrives home 19 May. His daughter Zdĕnka born 25 Sept. Concert tour of Germany and Holland fails owing to poor organization.	MacDowell born, 18 **Dec.**; Marschner (66) dies, 14 **Dec.**
1862	38	*Richard III* and *Wallenstein's Camp* performed to a minute audience. Bettina's second daughter Božena born, 19 Feb. Visits Göteborg for two months to teach and give recitals. At work on his first opera. Fails to become conductor of the Provisional Theatre, because he is thought to be a dangerous modernist.	Debussy born, 22 Aug.; Delius born, 29 Jan.; Halévy (62) dies, 17 March; Škroup (F.) (60) dies, 7 Feb.
1863	39	*The Brandenburgers* completed 23 April. Starts work on *The Bartered Bride*. Opens a music school with F. Heller. Becomes conductor of the Hlahol Choral Society.	Mascagni born, 7 Dec.
1864	40	Conducts *Haakon Jarl* (24 Feb.). Performs Berlioz's *Romeo and Juliet* at the Shakespeare tercentenary concert (23 April). Becomes music critic of *Národní listy* for one year. His subscription concerts are a failure.	Meyerbeer (72) dies, 2 May; Strauss (R.) born, 11 June.

Year	Age	Life	Contemporary Musicians
1865	41	*The Brandenburgers* is rehearsed, but Maýr, the conductor, is not interested in Smetana's work. Smetana begins sketching *Dalibor*. Applies for the directorship of the Conservatory, but is not appointed.	Dukas born, 1 Oct.; Glazunov born, 10 Aug.; Nielsen born, 9 June; Sibelius born, 8 Dec.
1866	42	Having done the final preparatory work, he conducts *The Brandenburgers*, which is a great success (5 Jan.). Wins Count Harrach's prize with this opera. *The Bartered Bride* is completed (15 March) and conducted by Smetana on 30 May, but the imminence of war keeps the audience away. Becomes principal conductor of the Provisional Theatre and conducts *Der Freischütz* on the first night (28 Sept.).	Busoni born, 1 April; Satie born, 17 May.
1867	43	Quarrel with Balakirev over *A Life for the Czar*. Completes *Dalibor* (29 Dec.).	Granados born, 27 July.
1868	44	Represents Czech musicians when the National Theatre foundation stone is laid (16 May). The performance of *Dalibor* on the same evening leads to accusations of Wagnerism. Begins to think about his next opera, *Libuše*. Smetana is incensed by the persecution of critics of the Austrian government.	Bantock born, 7 Aug.; Berwald (71) dies, 3 April; Rossini (76) dies, 13 Nov.
1869	45		Berlioz (65) dies, 8 March; Dargomizhsky (55) dies, 17 Jan.; Loewe (72) dies, 20 April; Pfitzner born, 5 May; Roussel born, 5 April.
1870	46	Pivoda attacks Smetana in *Pokrok* (22 Feb.) for his alleged	Balfe (62) dies, 20 Oct.; Mercadante (75) dies, 17 Dec.;

Year	Age	Life	Contemporary Musicians
		monopoly in Czech opera, and for being an extreme Wagnerian (3 March). Smetana visits Munich and sees *Die Walküre* three times (July).	Moscheles (75) dies, 10 March; Novák born, 5 Dec.
1871	47	Fiasco of *The Bartered Bride* at St Petersburg (11 Jan.), due to hostile criticism. Smetana conducts *St John's Rapids* by Rozkošný (3 Oct.).	Auber (89) dies, 12 May; Thalberg (59) dies, 27 April.
1872	48	Pivoda declares that Czech composers should write simply. Reactionary elements try to oust Smetana from the conductorship of the theatre (Oct.), but his friends rally round. *Libuše* completed 12 Nov. Eighty-six theatre subscribers call for Smetana's dismissal (Dec.).	Moniuszko (53) dies, 4 June; Skriabin born, 6 Jan.; Vaughan Williams born, 12 Oct.
1873	49	Smetana is reappointed as conductor at an increased salary. Begins work on *The Two Widows* (16 July).	Rakhmaninov born, 1 April; Reger born, 19 March.
1874	50	Completes *The Two Widows* (15 Jan.). Pivoda attacks Smetana's administration, and is supported by Linhardt and Maýr. Smetana replies. A purulent ulcer (12 April) is followed by throat trouble and a body rash. Onset of deafness (28 July). Announcement that he must give up all work temporarily (15 Aug.). Tries various treatments. *Politik* makes a fresh attack on Smetana (Sept.). Smetana completely deaf (20 Oct.). Composes *Vyšehrad* and *Vltava* (Sept.–Dec.).	Blodek (39) dies, 1 May; Cornelius (49) dies, 26 Oct.; Holst born, 21 Sept.; Ives born, 20 Oct.; Schönberg born, 13 Sept.; Suk born, 4 Jan.

Year	Age	Life	Contemporary Musicians
1875	51	*Šárka* composed (Jan.-20 Feb.). Countess Kaunitz arranges a concert to raise money for Smetana. *Vyšehrad* performed and encored (14 March). Successful performance of *Vltava* (4 April). 1,244 gulden raised for him by his Swedish friends. Travels to Würzburg (April) and Vienna (May) to consult specialists. His doctor prescribes a month of silence and isolation. *From Bohemia's Fields and Forests* completed 18 Oct. Begins work on *The Kiss*.	Bizet (36) dies, 3 June; Glière born, 11 Jan.; Ravel born, 7 March.
1876	52	Theatre Association in arrears with Smetana's salary, which forces him to leave Prague and settle with his daughter at Jabkenice (3 June). *The Kiss*, completed 31 Aug., is a great success (7 Nov.). *From Bohemia's Fields and Forests* performed 10 Dec. Smetana is unable to compose for more than an hour at a time. String quartet *From My Life* finished 29 Dec.	Falla born, 23 Nov.; Goetz (35) dies, 3 Dec.; Wolf-Ferrari born, 12 Jan.
1877	53	Composes *Songs of the Sea* (Jan.) and first part of *Czech Dances* (April). *Šárka* performed (17 March). Begins sketch of *The Secret*. Salary in arrears again, and no money left. Sacrifices royalties on *The Kiss* to obtain a new agreement with the theatre.	Dohnányi born, 27 July; Karg-Elert born, 21 Nov.
1878	54	Completes *The Secret* during the summer, and this is performed on 18 Sept., but Smetana is allowed only one benefit night. Completes *Tábor* (13 Dec.).	

Year	Age	Life	Contemporary Musicians
1879	55	Completes the cycle of symphonic poems *My Fatherland* with *Blaník* (9 March). Watches the first performance of his quartet through opera glasses. Writes ten more *Czech Dances*. Receives the libretto of *The Devil's Wall*, but his progress on the opera is slow.	Ireland born, 13 Aug.; Respighi born, 9 July.
1880	56	Concert in Prague to commemorate the fiftieth anniversary of his first public appearance; the two new symphonic poems are performed and Smetana plays in his Piano Trio (4 Jan.). Sketch of first act of *The Devil's Wall* finished (16 Feb.). *Vyšehrad* and *Vltava* published in full score.	Bloch born, 24 July; Medtner born, 5 Jan.; Offenbach (61) dies, 5 Oct.; Pizzetti born, 20 Sept.; Wieniawski (44) dies, 2 April.
1881	57	First act of *The Devil's Wall* completed in full score (12 March). Attends rehearsals of *Libuše*. This is performed (11 June) at the official opening of the National Theatre. The new theatre destroyed by fire (12 Aug.). Second act of *The Devil's Wall* completed (15 Sept.). Hamburg performance of *The Two Widows* upsets Smetana because of unauthorized alterations (28 Dec.).	Bartók born, 25 March; Miaskovsky born, 20 April; Mussorgsky (42) dies, 28 March; Vieuxtemps (61) dies, 6 June.
1882	58	The one hundredth performance of *The Bartered Bride* (5 May) is celebrated with a banquet. Having finished *The Devil's Wall* (June), Smetana starts on a second String Quartet, but encounters greater difficulties than before. The new opera is given an inadequate	Kodály born, 16 Dec.; Malipiero born, 18 March; Raff (60) dies, 24–5 June; Stravinsky born, 17 June; Szymanowsky born, 6 Oct.; Turina born 9 Dec.

Year	Age	Life	Contemporary Musicians
		first performance (29 Oct.) and Smetana's benefit night is disastrous. The complete cycle *My Fatherland* is a triumph (5 Nov.). Loses his memory and power of speech twice, and is told to close his mind to music.	
1883	59	Finishes his second String Quartet (12 March). Writes the Introduction and Polonaise for a symphonic suite, but makes no progress after 14 Sept. Suffers from hallucinations. *Libuše* is performed at the newly built National Theatre (18 Nov.).	Bax born, 8 Nov.; Flotow (70) dies, 24 Jan.; Wagner (69) dies, 13 Feb.; Webern born, 3 Dec.
1884	60	Makes pathetic attempts to write another opera, *Viola*, while signs of insanity increase. Is transferred to an asylum in Prague, 23 April, where he dies on 12 May.	Albeniz 24; Alkan 71; Balakirev 47; Bantock 16; Bartók 3; Bax 1; Bendl 46; Bloch 4; Boito 42; Borodin 51; Brahms 51; Bruch 46; Bruckner 60; Busoni 18; Chabrier 43; Chausson 29; Cui 49; Debussy 22; Delibes 48; Delius 22; d'Indy 33; Dohnányi 7; Dukas 19; Duparc 36; Dvořák 43; Elgar 27; Falla 8; Fauré 39; Fibich 34; Foerster 25; Franck 62; Franz 69; Gade 67; Glazunov 19; Glière 9; Goldmark 53; Gounod 66; Granados 17; Grieg 41; Henselt 70; Holst 10; Humperdinck 30; Ireland 5; Ives 10; Janáček 30; Karg-Elert 7; Kodály 2; Lalo 61; Lecocq 52; Leoncavallo 26; Liszt 73; MacDowell 23; Mahler 24; Malipiero 2; Mascagni 21; Massenet 42; Medtner 5; Miaskovsky 3; Nielsen 19; Novák 14; Parry 36;

Year	Age	Life	Contemporary Musicians

Pedrell 43; Pfitzner 15; Pizzetti 4; Puccini 26; Rakhmaninov 11; Ravel 9; Reger 11; Reinecke 60; Respighi 5; Rimsky-Korsakov 40; Roussel 15; Rozkošný 51; Rubinstein 55; Saint-Saëns 49; Satie 18; Schönberg 10; Šebor 41; Sibelius 19; Sinding 28; Skriabin 12; Skuherský 54; Stanford 32; Strauss (J. ii) 59; Strauss (R.) 20; Stravinsky 2; Suk 10; Sullivan 42; Svendsen 44; Szymanovsky 2; Taneyev 28; Tchaikovsky 44; Thomas (A.) 73; Turina 2; Vaughan Williams 12; Verdi 71; Vojáček 59; Webern 1; Wolf 24; Wolf-Ferrari 8.

APPENDIX B

I. OPERAS

1862–3	*The Brandenburgers in Bohemia* 3 acts (K. Sabina)	Provisional Theatre 5 Jan. 1866
1863–6	*The Bartered Bride* (*Prodaná nevěsta*) First two versions, 2 acts; third and fourth versions, 3 acts (K. Sabina)	Provisional Theatre 30 May 1866
1865–7	*Dalibor* 3 acts (J. Wenzig—E. Špindler)	New Town Theatre 16 May 1868
1869–72	*Libuše* 3 acts (J. Wenzig—E. Špindler)	National Theatre 11 June 1881
1873–4	*The Two Widows* (*Dvě vdovy*) 2 acts (E. Züngl)	Provisional Theatre 27 March 1874
1875–6	*The Kiss* (*Hubička*) 2 acts (E. Krásnohorská)	Provisional Theatre 7 Nov. 1876
1877–8	*The Secret* (*Tajemství*) 3 acts (E. Krásnohorská)	New Czech Theatre 18 Sept. 1878
1879–82	*The Devil's Wall* (*Čertova stěna*) 3 acts (E. Krásnohorská)	New Czech Theatre 29 Oct. 1882
1884	*Viola* Fragment (E. Krásnohorská)	

II. CHORAL WORKS
i. *Male Voice Choir, unaccompanied*

Czech Song (*Píseň česká*), Jan z Hvězdy (i.e. J. J. Marek) 1860.
The Three Riders (*Tři jezdci*), J. V. Jahn, 1862.
The Renegade (*Odrodilec*), A. Metliński, trans. F. L. Čelakovský, double chorus, 1863.
The Renegade, solo quartet and chorus, 1864.
Farming (*Rolnická*), V. Trnobranský, 1868.
Ceremonial Chorus (*Slavnostní sbor*), E. Züngl, 1870.

Song of the Sea (Píseň na moři), V. Hálek, 1877.
Dedication (Věno), J. Srb-Debrnov, 1880.
Prayer (Modlitba), J. Srb-Debrnov, 1880.
Motto (Heslo), J. Srb-Debrnov, two settings, 1882.
Our Song (Naše píseň), J. Srb-Debrnov, 1883.

ii. *Female Voices* (S.S.A.)

My Star (Má hvězda), B. Peška, 1878.
Return of the Swallows (Přiletěly vlaštovičky), J. V. Sládek, 1878.
The sun sets behind the mountain (Za hory slunce zapadá), J. V. Sládek, 1878.

iii. *Mixed Choir*

(a) Unaccompanied
Heilig ist der Herr Zebaoth (Psalm 117), double choir, 1846.

(b) With piano accompaniment
Czech Song (Česká píseň), Jan z Hvězdy, 1868.

(c) With orchestra
Two Offertories, 1846.
  'Scapulis suis obumbrabit tibi Dominus'
  'Meditabitur in mandatis tuis'
Czech Song (Česká píseň), Jan z Hvězdy, 1878.

iv. *Unison Song*

Song of Freedom (Píseň svobody), J. J. Kolár, 1848.

III. SONGS

Liebchen's Blick, B. Breiger, 1846.
Lebewohl, W. Melhop, 1846.
Schmerz der Trennung, C. M. Wieland, 1846.
Einladung, J. G. Jacobi, 1846.
Liebesfrühling, F. Rückert, 1853.
O Gustave, můj králi (O Gustav, my king), E. Bozděch, 1867. Song for the tragedy *Baron Goertz*.
Evening Songs (Večerní písně), V. Hálek, 1879.
  1. 'Kdo v zlaté struny zahrát zná'
  2. 'Nekamenujte proroky!'
  3. 'Mně zdálo se: "bol sestár' už . . ."'
  4. 'Hej, jaká zadost v kole'
  5. 'Z svých písní trůn Ti udělám'

IV. ORCHESTRAL WORKS

Menuetto in B flat major, 1842.
Galop Bajaderek, 1842.
Overture in D major for full orchestra, 1848–9.
Triumphal Symphony, 1853.
Richard III, symphonic poem, 1858.
Wallenstein's Camp, symphonic poem, 1858–9.
Haakon Jarl, symphonic poem, 1860–1.
Doktor Faust, overture for a puppet play by M. Kopecký, 1862.
Oldřich and Božena, overture for a puppet play by M. Kopecký, 1863.
March for the Shakespearean Festival, 1864.
Fanfare for the play *Richard III*, 1867.
Ceremonial Prelude in C major, 1868.
Rybář (The Fisherman), music for a *tableau vivant* based on the poem by Goethe, 1869.
Libušin soud (Libuše's judgment), music for a *tableau vivant*, 1869.
Má vlast (My Fatherland), cycle of six symphonic poems.
   Vyšehrad, 1872–4.
   Vltava, 1874.
   Šárka, 1875.
   Z českych luhů a hájů (From Bohemia's Fields and Forests), 1875.
   Tábor, 1878.
   Blaník, 1879.
Venkovanka (Peasant Woman), polka for the Artistic Circle, 1879. (For version for piano solo, see section VI.)
Prague Carnival. Introduction and Polonaise for a symphonic suite, 1883.

V. CHAMBER MUSIC

Fantasia on the song 'Sil jsem proso na souvrati', for violin and piano, 1842.
Piano Trio in G minor, Op. 15, 1855.
String Quartet in E minor, *Z mého života* (From my life), 1876.
Z domoviny (From the homeland), for violin and piano, 1880.
Second String Quartet in D minor, 1882–3.

VI. PIANO MUSIC
i. *Piano Solo*

Opus no.
   —   *Louise's Polka*, 1840.
   —   *Jiřinková (Dahlia) Polka*, 1840.
   —   *Galopp di Bravoura*, 1840.
   —   *Impromptus*, 1841–2.
         E flat minor; B minor; A flat major.

Opus no.

— *From a Student's Life* (*Ze studentského života*), polka in C major, 1842; revised 1858.

— Quadrille in B flat major, *c.* 1843.

— Quadrille in F major, 1843.

— *Duet without words* (*Duo beze slov*), 1843.

— *Souvenir of Pilsen* (*Vzpomínka na Plzeň*), polka in E flat major, 1843.

— *Piece without title* (*Skladba bez názvu*), capricccio in mazurka style in C sharp minor, 1843.

— Waltz in five parts, 1844.

— *Bagatelles and Impromptus*, 1844.

'Innocence'   'Happiness'
'Dejection'   'Fairy tale'
'Idyll'   'Love'
'Longing'   'Quarrel'

— *Album Leaves* (*Lístecky do památníku*), 1844–5.

Moderato, B major   C minor
Allegro, A flat major   Lento, E flat minor
Agitato, E major

— *Pensée fugitive*, Andante in D minor, 1845.

— *Studies*, 1846.

C major (prelude)   A minor (song form)

— Characteristic Variations on the Czech folk-song 'Sil jsem proso na souvrati', 1846.

— Sonata in G minor, 1846.

— Polka in E flat major, 1846.

— Characteristic Piece in C flat major, 1847.

1 *Six Characteristic Pieces*, 1848.

'In the forest'   'Longing'
'Rising passion'   'The soldier'
'The shepherdess'   'Despair'

— Romance in B flat major, 1848.

— *March of the Prague Students' Legion* (*Pochod pražské studentské legie*), 1848.

— *March of the National Guard* (*Pochod národní gardy*), 1848.

— Caprice in G minor, 1848.

2 *Six Album Leaves,* 1849.

Preludium, C major   Allegro comodo, E minor
Chanson, A minor   Moderato con anima, D major
Vivace, G major   Andante ma non troppo, B minor

— *Album Leaves*, 1849. From Countess Elisabeth Thun's album.

Allegretto ma non troppo, B flat major

Opus no.

	Allegretto, A major (1st version of Scherzo-polka, op. 5).
—	*Album Leaves,* 1849.

Allegro, B minor   B flat minor
Allegro non tanto,   E flat minor
   G major
   G minor   Toccatina, Vivace, B flat major

—   Andante in E flat major, 1849. From the album for the Emperor
      Ferdinand.

3   *Album Leaves,* 1849.
      'To Robert Schumann', E major
      'Wayfarer's song' (Píseň pocestného), A major
      'Droning, hissing and whistling are heard here' ('Es siedet
      und braust . . .'). [Molto agitato], C sharp minor

4   *Sketches* (Črty), series I, 1849.
      'Preludium', F sharp   'Remembrance', A flat major
        minor   'Relentless struggle', G sharp
      'Idyll', B major   minor

5   *Sketches,* series II, 1849.
      'Scherzo-polka', F sharp   'Pleasant landscape', D flat major
        major   'Rhapsodie', F minor
      'Melancholy', G sharp
        minor

—   *Wedding Scenes (Svatební scény),* 1849.
      'Wedding procession'
      'Bride and bridegroom'
      'Wedding revels'

—   *Allegro capriccioso,* B minor, 1849.

—   *Woodland Sensations and Impressions (Lesní city a dojmy),* 1849–50.
      Impromptu in F minor, sub-titled 'Nocturne'.

—   *A Treasure of Melodies (Poklad melodií),* 1850.
      Preludium, C major
      Capriccio, A minor
      Vivace, G major
      Polka in C major, *c.* 1850–2.

—   Polka in E major, *c.* 1852–3.
—   Polka in G minor, *c.* 1852–3.
—   Polka in A major, *c.* 1852–3.

7   *Salon Polkas,* 1854.
      F sharp major; F minor; E major.

8   *Poetic Polkas,* 1854.
      E flat major; G minor; A flat major.

—   Polka in F minor, *c.* 1854.

Opus no.

—   *Vision at the Ball (Viděni na plese)*, 1858. In the form of a polka.
—   Concert Study in C major (Scherzo study), 1858.
—   *Macbeth and the Witches*, 1859.
—   *Betty's Polka*, C major, 1859; revised 1883.

12 and 13 *Memories of Bohemia*, in the form of polkas, 1859–60.
      I. Polka in A minor   Polka in E minor
      II. Polka in E minor   Polka in E flat major

17   Concert Study, *On the Seashore (Na břehu mořském)*, 1861.
—   *Album Leaf for Marie Proksch*, C major, 1862.
—   *Fantasia on Czech National Songs*, 1862.
—   *Dreams (Sny)*, 1875.
    'Bygone happiness'   'In Bohemia'
    'Consolation'   'Before the castle'
    'In the salon'   'Harvest home'
—   *Czech Dances*, part I, 1877. Polkas.
    F sharp minor; A minor; F major; B flat major.
—   *Czech Dances*, part II, 1879.
    'Furiant'   'Dupák'
    'Slepička'   'Hulán'
    'Oves'   'Obkročák'
    'Medvěd'   'Sousedská'
    'Cibulička'   'Skočná'
—   *Peasant Woman (Venkovanka)*, 1879. Polka for the National Association.
—   Andante in F minor, 1880.
—   *Romance*, 1881. Contribution to the Artistic Circle album.

ii. *Two pianos, eight hands*
—   Sonata in E minor, in one movement, 1849.
—   Rondo in C major, 1851.

iii. *Transcription*
Transcription of Schubert's song 'Der Neugierige' (*Die schöne Müllerin*), 1858.

APPENDIX C

Bendl, Karel (1838–97), Czech composer and conductor. Friend of Dvořák. He wrote operas, choral music, songs and other works. He conducted the Prague Hlahol Choral Society from 1865 to 1877, but also held posts in Brussels, Amsterdam, Paris and Milan. His operas include *Lejla*, *The Old Bridegroom*, *The Montenegrins* and *The Child of Tábor*.

Bull, Ole (1810–80), Norwegian violinist and composer. He claimed that hearing Paganini play in Paris in 1831 was the turning point in his career. Had great success in Italy, and later played in many parts of Europe and earned a fine reputation in North America. He helped to establish a Norse theatre at Bergen and attempted to found a Norwegian colony in Pennsylvania.

Čech, Adolf (1841–1903), Czech conductor. His real name was Tausík. He was chorus master at the Provisional Theatre, and Smetana's assistant conductor from 1866 to 1874. He became principal conductor and was the first conductor of the National Theatre. He conducted the first performance of *Libuše* and Smetana's last three operas, and also the first complete performance of *My Fatherland*.

Czapek, Josef (1825–1915), Czech violinist and composer. He conducted concerts in Berlin for three seasons, and in 1847 settled permanently at Göteborg. He was organist of both the synagogue and the English church for fifty years, director of chamber concerts, conductor of the Harmonic Society orchestra and of the German opera, and was a member of the Swedish Academy of Music.

Dreyschock, Alexander (1818–69), Czech pianist. A pupil of Tomášek, he achieved international fame in 1838. He was a professor at the St Petersburg Conservatory and imperial court pianist from 1862. He left Russia for Italy in 1868 and died in Venice.

Erben, Karel Jaromír (1811–70), archivist of the city of Prague and poet. Collected more than two thousand folk poems and over eight hundred folk and nursery songs, the first of which were published in *Písně národní v*

Čecháh (1842–5). He was editor of *Pražské noviny* (Prague News) during the Revolution, and in 1853 published *Kytice z pověstí národních* (A Bouquet of Folk Tales), from which Dvořák took *The Spectre's Bride* and other ballads.

Fibich, Zdeněk (1850–1900), Czech composer. Taught at Vilna and became assistant conductor at the Provisional Theatre (1875–8), after which he devoted himself entirely to composition. He wrote in most available forms and was greatly interested in melodrama. Composed the great melodramatic trilogy *Hippodamie* (1889–91).

Hálek, Vítězslav (1835–74), Czech poet and journalist. Edited the almanac *Maj*. A greatly respected public figure whose best poems are his short lyrics, *Večerní písně* (Evening Songs) and *V přírodě* (Amid Nature). All his wisdom and charm are acknowledged to stem from nature.

Havlíček (Borovský), Karel (1821–56), Czech poet, journalist, editor and radical nationalist. While a tutor in Russia he realized that all hopes for Pan-Slav unity were futile, and that the Czechs could only win independence from Austria by their own efforts.

Heller, Ferdinand (1824–1912), Czech conductor, composer and violinist. Studied under Hellmesberger in Vienna. Took part in the demonstration against the Austrian police state in Prague in 1860. He was active in Prague musical life for many years.

Herbeck, Johann (1831–77), Austrian conductor and composer. Held a series of important positions as conductor in Vienna, including at the *Gesellschaft der Musikfreunde* concerts (1859 and 1875), as chief court Kapellmeister (1866) and as director of the court opera (1871). He was awarded the Iron Crown, third class.

Hostinský, Otakar (1847–1910), Czech aesthete and writer on music. After gaining a doctorate at Munich University he became the music critic of several influential journals. Became lecturer (1877) and later full professor (1892) of aesthetics at Charles University, Prague, and published books on Herbartian philosophy.

Jungmann, Josef (1773–1847), Czech poet, philologist and translator. Built upon the foundations of Czech philology laid by Josef Dobrovský (1753–1829). His crowning achievement was his *Dictionary of the Czech Language*, which played an important rôle in the revival of the Czech tongue.

Kittl, Jan Bedřich (1806–68), Czech composer and conductor. Studied law, but turned to music. Succeeded Dionys Weber as director of the Prague Conservatory in 1843, and retired twenty-two years later. He was a friend of Liszt, Berlioz and Wagner. He had an early success with his *Hunting Symphony* (1838).

Kolár, Josef Jiří (1812–96), Czech actor, producer and poet. Uncle of Smetana's first wife. The chosen representative of the acting profession and drama when the National Theatre foundation stone was laid. On that day he read his *Prophecy of Libuše*.

Kömpel, August (1831–91), German violinist. A pupil of Spohr. After being a member of the orchestras at Kassel and Hanover, he became leader of the Weimar orchestra (1863), a post he held for twenty-one years.

Krejčí, Josef (1821–81), Czech musical pedagogue and composer. Director of the Prague Organ School (1858). After being acting-director of the Prague Conservatory, he became director in 1866 and continued in office until his death. He had a strictly classical musical outlook.

Lachner, Ferdinand (1856–1910), Czech violinist. Studied with Bennewitz at the Prague Conservatory, where he became a professor in 1891. He was leader of the National Theatre orchestra from 1883, and toured with Dvořák and Wihan (cellist) in 1892.

Laub, Ferdinand (1832–75), Czech violinist. An infant prodigy who attracted the attention of Berlioz and Liszt (1846). Succeeded Joachim as leader of the Weimar orchestra (1853), and then moved to Berlin (1855). He was leading violin professor at the Moscow Conservatory (1866–74) and leader of the orchestra and string quartet of the Russian Musical Society. His reputation both as a teacher and a performer was very great.

Maýr, Jan Nepomuk (1818–88), Czech conductor. Principal of the Prague School of Singing from 1854. Became the first conductor of the Provisional Theatre (1862–6), and resumed this position when deafness forced Smetana to resign in 1874.

Moniuszko, Stanisław (1819–72), Polish composer. Studied in Berlin, where he was influenced by choral music and by Spontini's opera performances. *Halka* (1848) is his most popular opera, but *The Haunted Manor* (1865) is considered to be finer. His choral compositions have great merit.

Mottl, Felix (1856–1911), Austrian conductor and composer. While a student at the Vienna Conservatory he won all the available prizes. Made his name as conductor of the grand-ducal opera house at Carlsruhe (1881–1903). Conducted Wagner's *Ring* at Covent Garden in 1898, and in 1907 he became director of the Munich opera.

Nápravník, Eduard (1839–1916), Czech conductor and composer, who adopted Russian citizenship. In 1861 he went to Russia to conduct Prince N. Yussupov's private orchestra. Became assistant conductor of the imperial opera, St Petersburg, in 1867, and from 1869 until his death he was chief conductor. Gave the first performance of *Boris Godunov* (1874) and many other important works.

Neruda, Jan (1834–91), Czech poet, journalist and critic. Firmly believed that Czech art must reflect the spirit of the nation. His *Tales of Malá Strana* (1878) present vivid studies of Prague characters and are concerned with the social problems of the time.

Novotný, Václav Juda (1849–1922), Czech writer on music and composer. Contributed articles to *Dalibor* and other leading journals on various subjects, including reminiscences of Smetana. He accompanied Dvořák on his second visit to England (1884).

Palacký, František (1798–1876), Czech historian and political leader. Author of the monumental five-volume *History of the Czech People* (1836–67), which is the standard work on this subject up to the end of independence in 1526. Acknowledged leader of the party striving for a federal kingdom of Bohemia, Moravia and Silesia.

Pivoda, František (1824–98), Czech professor of singing and journalist. Studied in Vienna and then became singing teacher to Prince R. Khevenhüller's family (1853–60). Founded his own school of singing in Prague (1869). Editor of *Hudební listy* (1874–5).

Pollini, Bernhard (1838–97), German impresario. His real name was Baruch Pohl. Began his career as a baritone singer at the Cologne opera (1858). He became director of the municipal theatre, Hamburg, in 1874, just after it had been rebuilt.

Procházka, Jan Ludevít (1837–84), Czech pianist, critic, impresario and composer. Doctor of jurisprudence. Studied piano and theory with Smetana. He was music critic of *Národní listy* for twelve years, and editor of *Hudební listy* (1870–2) and *Dalibor* (1873–5). He became professor of piano at the Hamburg Conservatory in 1879, and conductor of that city's orchestral association.

Proksch, Josef (1794–1864), Czech musical pedagogue. Completely blind from the age of seventeen. Opened his own school of music in 1830, and counted Karel Slavkovský, Jindřich Kàan and Smetana among his pupils. Organized soirées and concerts. Published a treatise of pianoforte playing in fifty parts (1841–64).

Rieger, František Ladislav (1818–1903), Czech statesman and lawyer. The leading member of the *staročeši* (Old Czech Party). Intendant of the Provisional Theatre during the years 1866–76.

Rozkošný, Josef Richard (1833–1913), Czech composer. The most successful of his eleven operas were *St John's Rapids* (1871) and *Cinderella* (1885), which was the first Czech fairy-tale opera. He composed two symphonic poems, a *Fantastic Scherzo* and various other works.

Šebor, Karel Richard (1843–1903), Czech composer and conductor. He held conducting posts at several opera houses and for twenty years was an infantry bandmaster. His *Templars in Moravia* (1865) preceded Smetana's first opera by one year. This was followed by *Drahomíra* (1867) and *The Hussite Bride* (1868). Besides his five operas, he wrote symphonies, overtures and choral works.

Skuherský, František Zdeněk (1830-92), Czech composer, theorist and pedagogue. Having done important work as a conductor at Innsbruck (1854-1866), he became principal of the Prague Organ School (1866-90). He wrote a series of important text books and much church music. His three operas, which include *Vladimír, God's Chosen One* and *Lora*, were written to German libretti and subsequently translated into Czech.

Slanský, Ludvig (1838-1905), Czech conductor. Rose to be principal conductor of the Estates Theatre, Prague (1868), and then became conductor of the Prague German opera (1871-89). Shared the conductorship of the Philharmonic concerts with Smetana (1873-4). He was especially noted for his interpretations of *Die Meistersinger* and Beethoven's ninth symphony.

Srb-Debrnov, Josef (1836-1904), Czech writer on music. Studied Slavonic philology at Charles University, Prague. He was a singer and an amateur cellist. He was exceptionally active in organizing concerts of the Prague Hlahol Choral Society. Published *A History of Czech and Moravian Music* (1891), various articles for *Dalibor*, and *From the Diaries of Bedřich Smetana* (1901).

Šubert, František Adolf (1849-1915), Czech author and dramatist. Chiefly remembered for his liberal rule as first director of the Prague National Theatre (1883-1900), his support for Smetana and his music, and his enterprise in taking the theatre company to the International Music and Theatre Exhibition at Vienna (1892), where they performed *The Bartered Bride*. This was the prelude to this opera's world success.

Wenzig, Josef (1807-75), Czech writer and teacher. Headmaster of a leading Prague secondary school. Although he was educated and wrote in German, he had Czech and Slavonic sympathies. He was the first president of the *Umělecká beseda* (Artistic Circle).

Zelený, Václav Vladimír (1858-92), Czech editor and writer on music. Studied at Prague and Vienna universities, gaining a doctorate in jurisprudence. He was a pupil of J. B. Foerster for music theory. Contributed to various journals and edited *Dalibor* (1886-7). His Smetana articles were reprinted posthumously in book form.

APPENDIX D

BIBLIOGRAPHY

The following selective list includes the most important source material, almost all of which is in the Czech language. For additional sources, see the footnotes in the main part of this book. Smetana's diaries and a Smetana thematic catalogue are due to be published before long.

Balthasar, V., 'Bedřich Smetana' (Prague, 1924). Part I: a study of the personality and work from a psychological and psychopathological standpoint; Part II: Smetana's letters to Srb-Debrnov.

Bartoš, F., 'Smetana ve vzpomínkách a dopisech' (Prague 1939, 1941, 1948, 1954). The German translation (1954) gives the original text of the German documents. English translation: 'Bedřich Smetana: Letters and Reminiscences' (1955).

——, 'Příspěvky k soupisu dopisů Bedřicha Smetany', in *Hudební Věda* I, 4 (Prague, 1964), pp. 645–82. Additions and corrections to Očadlík's catalogue of letters.

Bartoš, F., and *Němec, Z.*, 'Z dopisů Bedřicha Smetany' (Prague, 1947). A selection of forty letters.

Bráfova, L., 'Rieger, Smetana, Dvořák' (Prague, 1915). Reminiscences.

Čeleda, J., 'Smetanův druh sděluje. Zivot a dílo Josefa Srba-Debrnova' (Prague, 1945). Smetana's companion communicates.

Clapham, J., 'Antonín Dvořák: Musician and Craftsman' (London and New York, 1966).

——, 'The Smetana-Pivoda Controversy', in *Music and Letters*, vol. 52, no. 4 (1971), pp. 353–64.

Dolanský, L., 'Hudební pamětí' (Prague, 1918, 1949). Musical memoirs.

Feldmann, H., 'Die Krankheit Friedrich Smetanas in otologische Sicht auf Grund neuer Quellenstudien', in *Monatsschrift für Ohrenheilkunde und Laryngo-Rhinologie*, vol. 98, no. 5 Vienna, 1964), pp. 209–26. English translation, *Music Review*, vol. 32, no. 3 (1971), pp. 233–47.

Helfert, V., 'O Smetanovi' (Prague, 1950). Essays.

Hostinský, O., 'Bedřich Smetana a jeho boj o moderní českou hudbu' (Prague, 1901, 1941). Smetana's struggle for modern Czech music.

Humlová, H., ed., 'Smetanova "Má vlast"' (Brno, 1939). Essays on *My Fatherland* by leading authorities.

Jarka, V. H., 'Kritické dílo Bedřicha Smetany 1858–1865' (Prague, 1948). Complete collection of Smetana's critical writings.

Jiránek, Jaroslav, 'Liszt a Smetana', in *Hudebni. věda,* 1961, no. 4, pp. 22–80. A comparison of their pianoforte styles.

Jiranek, Josef, 'Smetanův žák vzpomíná' (Prague, 1941). Smetana's pupil remembers. Includes letters. Reprinted as 'Vzpomínky a korespondence s Bedřichou Smetanou' (Prague, 1957).

Krásnohorská, E., 'Bedřich Smetana. Nástin života i působeni jeho uměleckého' (Prague, 1885, 1924). A fuller version of her article in *Osvěta* (1880). Early source material by Smetana's librettist. Reprinted in a critical edition in *Výbor z díla II* (1956).

Kraus, A., 'Smetana v Göteborgu', in *Věstník český akademie* (Prague, 1906). Smetana in Göteborg. The reprint (Prague, 1925) no longer includes the original text of German letters.

Kredba, O., 'Klavírní trio Bedřicha Smetany' (Prague, 1944).

Large, B., 'Smetana' (London, 1970).

Löwenbach, J., 'Bedřich Smetana a dr. Ludevít Procházka. Vzájemná Korespondence' (Prague, 1914). Letters.

Nejedlý, Z., 'Zpěvohry Smetanovy' (Prague, 1908, 1954). Smetana's operas.

Němeček, Jan, 'Nástin, české hudby XVIII století' (Prague, 1955). The most reliable book on eighteenth-century Czech music.

Newmarch, R., 'Smetana, Bedřich', in *Cobbett's Cyclopedic Survey of Chamber Music,* vol. ii (London, 1929, 1963), pp. 425–32.

Očadlík, M., 'Soupis dopisů Bedřicha Smetany', *Miscellanea musicologica,* vol. 15 (Prague, 1960). Chronological catalogue of letters.

—— 'Eliška Krásnohorská—Bedřich Smetana' (Prague, 1940). Letters.

—— 'Libuše. Vznik Smetanovy zpěvohry' (Prague, 1939, 1950). A detailed study of the subject and music of *Libuše*.

—— 'Klavírní dílo Bedřicha Smetany' (Prague, 1961). Handbook to the complete recordings of the piano music.

Plavec, J., 'Smetanova tvorba sborova' (Prague, 1954). Smetana's choral music.

Pražák, P., 'Smetanovy zpěvohry' (Prague, 1948). Smetana's operas; 4 volumes.

—— 'Smetanova Prodaná nevěsta. Vznik a osudy díla' (Prague, 1962). Origin and destiny of *The Bartered Bride*.

Procházka, L., 'Slavná doba české hudby. Výbor z kritik a článku' (Prague, 1958). A selection from Procházka's articles and criticisms.

Rutte, M., and *Sourek, O.* (eds.), 'Smetanův operní epilog' (Prague, 1942). Essays on *The Devil's Wall*.

Rychnovsky, E., 'Smetana' (Stuttgart and Berlin, 1924).

'Sborník Musea Bedřicha Smetany' (Prague, 1959). Smetana's appearance; catalogue of manuscripts; etc.

'Smetanův památník' (Hořice, 1903). Memorial volume of articles by contemporaries.

Šourek, O., Komorní skladby Bedřicha Smetany' (Prague, 1945). Smetana's chamber music.

—— 'Smetanova "Má vlast". Její vznik a osudy (Prague, 1940). The origin and destiny of *My Fatherland*.

Srb-Debrnov, J., 'Z deníku Bedřicha Smetany (1856–1861)' (Prague, 1902). From Smetana's diary.

Teige, K., 'Příspěvky k životopisu a umělecké činnosti Mistra B. Smetany.
    I. Skladby Smetanovy (Prague, 1893). Catalogue of works.
    II. Dopisy Smetanovy (Prague, 1896). Sixty-four letters, with the German letters given in their original text.

Thörnqvist, C., 'Smetana in Göteborg. 1856–1862' (Göteborg, 1967). In English.

Zelenka-Lerando, L., 'B. Smetana a E. Züngel' (Nymburk, 1903, 1905). Letters.

Zelený, V. V., 'O Bedřichu Smetanovi' (Prague, 1894). Reminiscences and broad analyses of *Libuše* and *The Devil's Wall*, etc.

Zich, O., 'Symfonické básně Smetanovy' (Prague, 1924, 1949). Smetana's symphonic poems.

APPENDIX E

The Post-Mortem Report, made by Professor Hlava on 13th May 1884, has been translated from the German original by the neurologist Dr Ernst Levin, who has also added a short explanation and commentary for the benefit of the lay reader.

REPORT

The body is that of a man of about sixty years of age, of small stature and with a fine bony structure, poorly nourished. The epidermis of the trunk is shrivelled, that of the face reddened as also is the mucosa of the lips. The conjunctivae, however, are pale. The neck is short and of adequate breadth. The thorax is flat and short and the abdomen sunken. There are abrasions around both knee caps. The skull is well proportioned, oval, 17 cm. long, 14 cm. wide, and about 1·5 cm. in thickness. Porosity is widespread. The inner surface is quite smooth, the periosteum pronounced tense and pale. In the sagittal sinus there is freshly clotted blood. There is thickening of the dura, most marked in the left frontal region, and also over the vertex where insignificant Pacchionian granulations are present. At the upper parts of the occipital lobes the soft parts of the brain are ill-defined [*fein*], the cerebral convolutions show differences from those of a normal brain. First of all they are strikingly broader and less numerous. The middle cerebral convolution, usually about 1 cm. wide, has a width of 2 cm. The third left cerebral gyrus (Broca's convolution) is especially broadened. The meninges lie very close to the brain surface and indeed cannot be separated from the thickened areas. On section it is found that the lateral ventricles are dilated and contain fluid. The ependyma is quite smooth and unaffected. The cortex everywhere is narrowed, being at the most 3 mm. thick, brownish, glistening and appears almost sclerosed. The basal ganglia are flattened but normal enough, the nucleus caudatus approximately 4 mm. (as opposed to the normal width of 2 mm.). The third ventricle is dilated, the ependyma thin, rough and pale. The small veins are wide and roughened. The fourth ventricle is dilated. The ependyma is coarse, granular, glistening and shows a brownish discoloration. The striae acousticae are inconspicuous, two on the right and

three only on the left. They are greyish and strikingly narrowed. The cere-
bellum is soft and pale. The pons and medulla oblongata are firm. The grey
matter is pigmented, as it is also in the spinal medullary prolongation. Both
auditory nerves are slender, greyish in colour and narrower than normal.
The veins [?] at the base of the brain are atheromatous. The weight of the
brain is 1250 grammes.

There is a lobular hepatisation in both lungs. The left side of the heart is
slightly enlarged. There is marked atheroma of the endocardium and almost
all the arteries. There is brown atrophy of the liver and kidneys. In the other
soft parts there is nothing especially abnormal to be noted. In the calcified
femoral artery there is a firmly adherent thrombus.

AUTOPSY DIAGNOSIS

Chronic leptomeningitis chiefly of the frontal lobes. Chronic porencephaly.
Chronic internal hydrocephalus. Red atrophy of the cerebrum (Atrophia
cerebri rubra). Granular ependymitis of the fourth ventricle, subsequent
atrophy of the acoustic striae. Atrophy of the acoustic nerves. Bilateral
lobular pneumonia. Widespread atrophy.

.   .   .   .   .   .

Friends of Smetana's music may ask two questions: did his illness demon-
strably influence the quantity and quality of his musical work; and could
his illness have been prevented, diagnosed earlier and treated more efficiently
if it had occurred today? The answer to the first question must be left to
musicians; the answer to the second may be attempted by medical men.

His illness was syphilis, which had been well known in Europe ever
since it was allegedly introduced from the New World by Christopher
Columbus about 1492.

The modern conception regarding the pathogenesis of this chronic
inflammatory disease has changed radically since the five-year period 1905–
1910: diagnostically by the demonstration of the causative organism and the
introduction by Wassermann of his serological reaction; and therapeutically
by the introduction by Paul Ehrlich of salvarsan.

At the time of the onset of Smetana's ear trouble, leading to total bilateral
deafness, the only specific treatment known to the medical world consisted
in the application of the dreaded *Schmierkur*, or cure by covering most of
the body with a mercurial ointment, which was very effective in many cases
in clearing the earlier symptoms. As regards the diagnosis, contemporary
physicians, including ear specialists and psychiatrists, seldom had any
doubt, since they relied on their own careful studies of the *clinical* course
of the disease, and on the excellent studies of the *pathological* findings
recorded whenever these were carried out, at a time when no specific
diagnostic tests were possible.

My tentative answer to the question whether the course and final outcome of both Smetana's ear condition and his final progressive mental condition would have been, or could have been, different in any significant and decisive way today is: probably not.

While it is true that the period 1905–10, with all its diagnostic and therapeutic advances, has certainly shed more light on our conception of the life history of syphilis inside the infected body at all stages—manifest or 'latent'—it cannot be said with any certainty that this period has altered the course of the disease and its final outcome in any predictable and 'scientifically reliable' way.

Edinburgh   ERNST LEVIN

INDEX

Abert, Jan Josef, 32
Ack Värmeland, du sköne, 80
Aerenthal, Baron L., 59
Alkan (C. H. V. Morhange), 60
Andrássy, Count Julius, 37
Andulka, mé dítě (folk-song), 108n
Auber, Daniel F. E., 12, 52
   La muette de Portici, 12
Aunt Pepi, 17

Bach, Alexander, 23, 28
Bach, Johann Sebastian, 27
   B minor Mass, 27
Balakirev, Mily Alexeievitch, 34–5
Bartoš, Prof. František, vii, 76, 95,
   99, 108
Beethoven, Ludwig van, 7, 15, 19,
   24, 25, 28, 29, 42, 56, 71
   Archduke Trio, Op. 97, 25, 29
   Ghost Trio, Op. 70, no. 2, 25
   Kreutzer Sonata, Op. 47, 28
   Piano Concerto in C minor, 25,
   29, 30
   Piano Trio, Op. 1, no. 1, 30
   Sonata for Piano in A flat, Op.
   26, 19
   Sonata for Violin and Piano in
   A minor, Op. 23, 30
   Sonata for Violin and Piano in G
   major, Op. 30, no. 3, 30
   Wind Quintet, Op. 16, 19
Bellini, Vincenzo, 15
Benda, František, 4
Benda, George (Jiří), 4–5, 8
Benda family, 4

Bendl, Karel, 35, 38, 40, 42, 46, 142
   Břetislav, 35
   Lejla, 35, 38
Benecke, Fröjda, 25, 28, 45, 60
Bennewitz, Antonín, 68
Berlioz, Hector, 5, 18–19, 32, 67,
   81, 116
   King Lear, 19
   Romeo and Juliet, 19, 32, 81
   Symphonie fantastique, 19, 67
Biber, Heinrich J. F. von, 3
Blahoslav, Jan, 2
Blodek, Vilém, 35
   In the Well, 35
Bohemia (periodical), 19
Bonuš, František, 70n
Book of Psalms and Sacred Songs
   (Comenius), 2
Borovský. *See* Havlíček, Karel
Bozděch, E., 88, 137
Brahms, Johannes, 122
Breiger, B., 137
Břetislav, 103
Bubeníček, 45
Budden, Julian, 73
Bull, Ole, 28, 142
Bülow, Hans von, 27
Burghauser, Jarmil, vii, 34n
Butula, František, 14, 16

Cameron, Dr E. H., vii
Čech, Adolf, 34n, 42, 47, 49, 53,
   74, 100, 109, 112n, 142
Čelakovský, F. L., 136
Černý, František, 11

Červinková, Marie, 51
Charles IV, 103
Cherubini, Luigi, 7, 32
  The Water Carrier, 7, 32
Chmelenský, Josef Krasoslav, 7
Chmelík, Jan, 12
Chopin, Frederic, 15, 19, 50, 57, 58
  Nocturne in B major, 50
  Preludes, 58
Čizek, Dr Antonín, 40, 43
Collorado, Archbishop Hierony-mous, 12n
Columbus, Christopher, 151
Comenius, Jan Ámos, 2
Constantine. *See* Cyril
Crown Prince of Austro-Hungarian Empire. *See* Rudolf, Crown Prince
Cyril, 1
Czapek, Josef, 24, 25, 26, 30, 142
Czernin, Count Prokop Adalbert, 12n
Czernin von Chudenitz, Count Johann Rudolf, 12–13
Czerny, Carl, 15

Dalayrac, Nicolas, 7
Dalibor (periodical), 42
Dickson, Eleonore, 23
Dietrichstein, Prince Franz Josef, 10
Dobrovský, Josef, 6
Doležálek, Jan Emanuel, 6
Dorůžka, Dr Lubomír, vii
Doucha, 7
Dreyschock, Alexander, 23, 59, 142
Dušek, František Xaver, 4
Dusík, Jan Ladislav, 5
Dussek, J. L. *See* Dusík, J. L.
Dvořák, Antonín, 4, 40, 51, 52n, 66, 68–9, 81n, 89, 116, 118n, 122

Dimitrij, 51–2
String Quartet in A flat, Op. 105, 68–9
String Quartet in F, Op. 95, 68
String Quartet in G, Op. 106, 68
String Quintet in E flat, Op. 97, 66

Elisabeth of Bavaria, 22
Eliška, 101
Erben, Karel Jaromír, 142–3
Erlich, Paul, 151

Famintsin, Alexander Sergeyevitch, 38
Fels, Roderich, 52
Ferdinand I, 2
Ferdinand, Archduke, 5
Ferdinand, Emperor of Austria, 21, 32
Ferdinandová, Bettina. *See* Smeta-nová, Bettina
Fibich, Zdeněk, 4, 40, 81n, 89, 122, 143
Field, John, 6
Fils, Antonín. *See* Filtz, Anton
Filtz, Anton, 4
Fiske, Dr Roger, 72
Franck, César, 5
Franz II, Emperor, 12
Franz Josef, Emperor, 21–2, 23, 28, 37, 38, 71, 99
Frederick the Great, 4
Frederick, Crown Prince. *See* Frederick the Great
Frederick III, Duke, 4
furiant, 64, 95, 116
Fux, Johann Joseph, 5

Gade, Niels W., 25, 27
  The Elf King's Daughter, 25
Gassmann, Florian Leopold, 5
George of Poděbrady, 101

Index

Glinka, Mikhail Ivanovitch, 33, 34, 122
    Kamarinskaya, 33
    A Life for the Czar, 34
    Ruslan and Lyudmila, 35
Gluck, Christoph Willibald, 26
    Orfeo, 26
Gorer, Richard, 106
Gounod, Charles F., 5
Grieg, Edvard H., 59
Grosse, 29
Gyrowetz, Adalbert, 5, 8, 11

Haakon, Earl of Lade, 73, 75
Hagen, Dr, 46
Hálek, Vitězslav, 32, 48, 87, 88, 137, 143
Hallberger, 58
Hanka, Vácslav, 6
Harald Graafeld, 75
Harant of Polžice, Kryštof, 2
Harmoniska Sällskapet, 24, 26, 28
Harrach, Count Jan von, 31, 33
Havlíček, Karel, 14, 20, 22, 87, 143
Haydn, F. Joseph, 5, 11, 29, 67n, 71
    The Creation, 29
    'Emperor's Hymn', 71
Heller, Ferdinand, 32, 88, 143
Henselt, Adolf von, 60
Herbeck, Johann, 25, 143
Herder, Johann Gottfried von, 6
Hérold, L. J. Ferdinand, 14
Herz, Henri, 15
Hlahol Choral Society (Prague), 32, 48, 86
Hlava, Dr, 56, 150
Hoffmann, Jan, 19
Hohenwart, Count von, 37
Hostinský, Dr Otakar, 39, 40, 42, 54, 143
Hřimalý, Bohuslav, 40
Hudební listy (periodical), 40, 41, 42, 44

Hummel, Johann Nepomuk, 60
Hus, Jan, 86
Hussite Chorale. *See* 'Ye who are God's Warriors!'
Hymnal of Jistebnice, 2

Ikavec, František, 13

Jacobi, J. G., 137
Jahn, J. V., 86, 136
Jan z Hvězdy, 6, 29, 86, 136, 137
Janáček, Leoš, 81n
Jaroslav of Šternberk, 101
Jewess, The (Halévy), 42
Jiránek, Josef, 62
Jirovec, Adalbert. *See* Gyrowetz
Jitka, 103
Jungmann, Josef, 15, 143

Kalkbrenner, Friedrich W. M., 19, 60
Karel, J. V., 51
Kaunitz, Elizabeth (*née* Thun), 18, 45
Kdož jste Boží bojovníci. See 'Ye who are God's Warriors!'
Kistner, Franz, 20, 58
Kittl, Jan Bedřich, 18, 32, 33, 143
Kolár, Josef Jiří, 21, 31, 35, 137, 144
Kolář, Karel (brother-in-law), 13
Kolář, Karel (father-in-law), 13, 15
Kolářová, Anna (mother-in-law), 17–18, 26–7
Kolářová, Kateřina. *See* Smetanová, Kateřina
Komenský, Jan Ámos. *See* Comenius
Kömpel, August, 48, 143
Kopecký, O., 67n
Kossuth, Lájos, 21
Kostka, František, 16
Kott, František B., 7–8

Koželuh, Leopold, 5, 6
Krásnohorská, Eliška, 47, 48, 50, 51, 136
Krejčí, Josef, 33, 144
Krommer, František, 5

Lachner, Ferdinand, 144
Large, Brian, vii
Laub, Ferdinand, 28, 144
Lecocq, Alexandre Charles, 52
Leopold II, 10
Levin, Ernst, vii, 150, 152
Lichtenstein of Kastelkorn, Prince-Bishop Karel, 2
Linhardt, V., 41
Liszt, Franz, 5, 15, 16, 19–20, 23, 24, 25, 26, 27, 28, 29, 30, 48, 60, 65, 71, 73, 74, 96, 116
    Estergom Mass, 23, 27
    Faust Symphony, 25
    Hungarian Rhapsody, No. 1, 28
    Die Ideale, 25
    Mephisto Waltz, 62
    Rigoletto Fantasia, 29
Lortzing, G. Albert, 95
    Czar and Carpenter, 51, 95
Luke, Bishop, 2
Lynek, Jan (Smetana's maternal grandfather), 10
Lynek, Josef (Smetana's uncle), 12

Má mila, má mila, černé oči máte (folk-song), 116
Macháček, Simeon, 6, 7
Macourek, Jiří, 8
Mallefille, Félicien, 41
Malý, Dr Miroslav, vii
Marek, J. J. *See* Jan z Hvězdy
Mareš, Jan Antonín, 5
Marie-Antoinette, Empress, 5
Maťocha, Victorin, 13
Maýr, Jan Nepomuk, 32, 33, 34, 40, 41, 42, 47, 52, 54, 144

Měchura, Leopold Eugen, 35
Méhul, Étienne, 7
Meissner, August, 24, 25, 29
Melhop, W., 137
Mendelssohn-Bartholdy, Felix, 19, 24, 25, 30, 57, 71
    Elijah, 25, 28
    Piano Concerto in G minor, 30
    Piano Trio in D minor, 24
    St Paul, 26
    Songs Without Words, 19
Mernardi, Bartolomeo, 3
Messiah, 28
Methodius, 1
Metlinskij, A., 136
Metternich, Prince C. W. L. Metternich-Winneburg, 21
Miča, František Adam Jan, 5–6
Miča, František Václav, 7
Michna, Adam Václav, 3
Moniuszko, Stanisław, 35, 144
    Halka, 35
Monteverdi, Claudio, 101
Morzin, Count, 10
Moscheles, Ignaz, 60
Mottl, Felix, 49, 144
Mozart, Wolfgang Amadeus, 4, 5, 12–13, 16, 24, 26, 27, 56, 94
    Don Giovanni, 7
    Die Entführung aus dem Serail, 7
    The Magic Flute, 7
    The Marriage of Figaro, 94
    Piano Concerto in D minor, K.466, 26
    Requiem Mass, 27
Mysliveček, Josef, 5, 8

Napoleon III, 28
Nápravník, Eduard, 38, 144
Národní listy (newspaper), 32, 45
Naryshkin, Count, 5
National Theatre, 35, 38, 51, 52, 54, 99

Nejedlý, V., 6
Nejedlý, Zdeněk, vii, 11
Neruda, Jan, 45, 94, 145
Neue Zeitschrift für Musik, 27
Nissen, A., 25, 30
Nittinger, Dr Robert, 49
Nostitz family, 21
Novotný, Václav Juda, 25, 145

O Nederland! let op u saeck, 80
Oćadlík, Mirko, 59, 114
Offenbach, Jacques, 38, 52
Öhlenschläger, Adam, 28, 74, 75
Olaf Tryggvessön, 75
Onslow, Georges, 19
Osvěta (periodical), 40
Otakar II. *See* Přemysl Otakar II
Otto I, 1
Otto V, Burgrave of Brandenburg, 90–1

Paisiello, Giovanni, 7
Palacký, František, 21, 35, 145
Peška, B., 137
Pichl, Václav, 5
Pivoda, František, 33, 38–42, 145
Pixis, Johann Peter, 15
Pleyel, Ignaz J., 11
Pokrok (newspaper), 38
Politik (newspaper), 41, 44, 45
Politzer, Prof. Adam, 45
Pollini, Bernard, 52, 145
Pradácová, Ludmila, 16
Prague Conservatory, 33
Přemysl Otakar II, 90, 101
Procházka, Dr Ludevít, 28, 42, 49, 52, 145
Prokop the Great, 101
Proksch, Josef, 17–18, 19, 57, 145
Provisional Theatre, 31, 32, 34, 38

Rastislav, Prince, 1
Reicha, Antonín, 5, 8

Richard III, 72–3
Richter, Franz Xaver, 4
Richter, Jan, 18
Rieger, Dr F. Ladislav, 31–2, 33, 40, 51, 145
Rossini, Gioacchino, 51
The Barber of Seville, 7, 94
Otello, 7
Tancredi, 7
William Tell, 15, 26
Rousseau, Jean Jacques, 4, 6
Rozkošný, Josef Richard, 35, 40, 145
Mikuláš, 35
St John's Rapids, 35
Rückert, J. M. Friedrich, 88, 137
Rudolf, Crown Prince, 51
Rudolf, King of the Romans, 90–1
Ryba, Jakub Šimon Jan, 6
Rychnovsky, Ernst, vii
Rychnovský, Jiří, 2

Sabina, Karel, 31, 33, 91, 94, 136
Šamotulny Hymnal, 2
Schaffgotsch, Count Johann A., 9
Schäffle, Albert, 37
Schiller, J. C. Friedrich von, 28, 58n, 73
Schubert, Franz Peter, 7, 15, 19, 57, 60, 66
'Der Neugierige', 57, 60
Piano Trio in E flat, 19, 66
'Serenade', 19
Schumann, Clara, 19, 59
Schumann, Robert, 19, 24, 25, 26, 27, 57, 59, 65, 66, 116
Genoveva, 27
Paradise and the Peri, 26
Piano Quintet, 25
Schwarz, Josef (Smetana's son-in-law), 48
Schwarzová, Žofie (*née* Smetanová, daughter), 21, 25, 48

Index

Šebor, Karel Richard, 34, 35, 39, 145–6
  Blanka, 35
  Drahomíra, 35, 39
  The Hussite Bride, 35
  The Templars in Moravia, 34
Sedlák, sedlák (folk-song), 64, 95
Serov, Alexander, 27
Shakespeare, William, 32, 72, 108
  Richard III, 72
  Twelfth Night, 47
Šindelář, Father Karel, 14
skočná, 68, 94
Skrejšovský, 42
Škroup, František, 6, 7, 8, 29, 34
  The Tinker, 7
Škroup, Jan Nepomuk, 8, 35
  The Swedes in Prague, 35
Skuherský, František Zdeněk, 34, 35, 40, 90, 146
  Lora, 35
  Vladimír, God's Chosen One, 34, 90
Sládek, Josef Václav, 137
Sladkovský, Karel, 35
Slánský, Ludvík, 47, 146
Šlapák, Dr Kamíl, vii
Slavoj (periodical), 32
Smetana, Antonín (brother), 12, 13
Smetana, Bedřich
  WORKS
  CHAMBER MUSIC
  From the Homeland, violin and piano, 70
  Piano Trio in G minor, 22, 26, 27, 50, 65–6, 116, 118
  String Quartet in E minor, 'From My Life', 48, 50, 66–8
  String Quartet No. 2 in D minor, 53, 54, 68–70, 84, 114
  CHORAL MUSIC
  Ceremonial Chorus, 87
  Czech Song, 29, 49, 50, 86, 88, 101

  Dedication, 88
  Farming, 86
  Our Song, 88
  The Renegade, 33, 86
  The Return of the Swallows, 88
  Song of the Sea, 48, 87
  The Sun Sets Behind the Mountain, 88
  The Three Riders, 33, 86
  OPERAS
  The Bartered Bride, 33, 34, 38, 49, 52, 57, 64, 76, 93–5, 106, 116, 119
  The Brandenburgers in Bohemia, 31, 33, 34, 38, 48, 52, 90–3, 116–117
  Dalibor, 33, 35–6, 37, 38, 39, 40, 52, 60, 88, 95–9, 102, 107, 118, 120–1
  The Devil's Wall, 51, 52–3, 111–15
  The Kiss, 47, 49, 81, 106–8, 113n, 120
  Libuše, 37–8, 51, 53, 54, 59, 65, 75, 76, 78, 86, 88, 95, 99–103, 104, 107, 119
  The Secret, 48, 49, 92, 106, 108–111, 117
  The Two Widows, 40–1, 52, 104–106, 107, 118
  Viola (fragment), 47, 54, 55
  ORCHESTRAL MUSIC
  Blaník, 2, 49, 78, 83, 84, 118–19
  Doctor Faust Overture, 33, 75
  Festive Overture, 35, 71
  From Bohemia's Fields and Forests, 47, 77, 81–3, 121
  Haakon Jarl, 28, 32, 60, 74–5
  Má vlast. See My Fatherland
  March for the Shakespearean Festival, 32, 75
  My Fatherland, 44, 50, 53, 75–84, 99
  Oldřich and Božena Overture, 33

Overture in D major, 21, 71
Prague Carnival, 54, 84–5
Richard III, 26, 27, 30, 71–3
Šárka, 44, 47, 77, 81, 107
Tábor, 2, 49, 78, 83–4
Triumphal Symphony, 22, 23, 65, 71, 118, 120n
Vltava, 44, 47, 77, 80, 81, 120
Vyšehrad, 44, 47, 77, 78–80
Wallenstein's Camp, 26, 27, 28, 30, 60, 73–4, 96
PIANO MUSIC
Album leaves, 58–9
Allegro capriccioso, 23, 57, 59
Bagatelles and Impromptus, 57, 58n
Ballad in E minor, 60
Betty's Polka, 28
Capriccio in Mazurka Style, 57
Cid Ximena (incomplete), 57
Concert Study in C major, 60
Czech Dances I, 48, 63
Czech Dances II, 50, 63–4, 70, 119
Dreams, 62–3
'Es siedet und braust . . .', 58, 59
'Fairy Tale', 57
Fantasia on Czech National Songs, 57
Jiřinková Polka, 57
Macbeth and the Witches, 60–2
March of the National Guard, 21, 22
March of the Prague Students' Legion, 21
Memories of Bohemia, Opp. 12 and 13, 28, 60
'Der Neugierige' (transcription), 57
On the Seashore, Op. 17, concert study, 29, 60
Pensée fugitive, 57
Poetic Polkas, Op. 8, 59, 119
Polka in A minor, 50

Polka in C major (*c.* 1850–2), 25, 60
Polka in E flat major (1846), 58
Polka in G minor (*c.* 1852–3), 59
'Preludium' (*Sketches*, Op. 4), 59
'Preludium' (*A Treasure of Melodies*), 59
Rondo in C major (8 hands), 59
Salon Polkas, Op. 7, 59
'Scherzo Polka', 59
Six Album Leaves, Op. 2, 58
Six Characteristic Pieces, Op. 1, 19, 25, 58
Sketches, Opp. 4 and 5, 58
Sonata in E minor (8 hands), 59
Sonata in G minor, 18, 57–8, 66
'To Robert Schumann', 58, 59, 86, 101–2
A Treasure of Melodies, 59
Vision at the Ball, 25, 60
Waltz (1844), 57
Wayfarer's Song, 58, 59, 120n
Wedding Scenes, 59, 94
SONGS
Baron Goertz, song for, 88
Evening Songs, 50, 88, 89
Liebesfrühling, 88
Song of Freedom (unison), 21, 88
Smetana, František (father), 9–11, 12, 13, 14, 17, 24
Smetana, Prof. František (cousin), 15, 20
Smetana, Jan (great-great-uncle), 9
Smetana, Josef (uncle), 9
Smetana, Karel (brother), 12, 27
Smetana, Matej (great-grandfather), 9
Smetana, Petr (great-great-great-grandfather), 9
Smetana, Václav (grandfather), 9
Smetana, Václav (great-great-grandfather), 9
Smetana, Václav (uncle), 9

Smetanová, Albina (step-sister), 10

Smetanová, Anna (*née* Bartoničk-ová, father's first wife), 10

Smetanová, Anna (step-sister), 10

Smetanová, Barbora (*née* Lynková, mother), 10–11, 13

Smetanová, Barbora (sister), 12

Smetanová, Bedřiška (daughter), 21, 22, 66

Smetanová, Bettina (*née* Ferdi-nandová, second wife), 27, 28, 29, 33, 44, 49n, 60

Smetanová, Božena (daughter), 33

Smetanová, Františka (sister), 13

Smetanová, Františka (step-sister), 10

Smetanová, Gabriela Jelčinka (daughter), 21, 22

Smetanová, Johanna (great-grand-mother), 9

Smetanová, Kateřina (daughter), 22

Smetanová, Kateřina (*née* Kolářová, first wife), 13, 15, 17–18, 19, 21, 23, 25, 26–7

Smetanová, Klára (step-sister), 10

Smetanová, Ludmila (*née* Exnerová, father's second wife), 10

Smetanová, Ludmila (*née* Konárov-ská, grandmother), 9

Smetanová, Ludmila (*née* Strunová, great-great-grandmother), 9

Smetanová, Ludmila (step-sister), 10

Smetanová, Marie (step-sister), 10

Smetanová, Zděnka (daughter), 29

Smetanová, Žofie (daughter). *See* Schwarzová, Zofie

Smetanová, Žofie (step-sister), 10

Society for Classical Choral Music, 24

Šourek, Otakar, 66

Špindler, Ervín, 35, 37, 136

Srb-Debrnov, Josef, 44, 48, 53, 55, 66, 68, 69, 70, 72, 87, 94, 137, 146

Stamitz, Johann, 4

Štěpánek, Jan Nepomuk, 7

Strakatý, Dr Jan, 56

Strauss, Richard, 105

Intermezzo, 105

Šubert, František Adolf, 54, 146

Suchý, 50

Suk, Josef, 2

Švabinská, Zuzana, vii

Světla, Karolina, 47

Svoboda, Antonín, 14

Tausig, Carl, 60

Taxis, Count Hugo von, 48

Thalberg, Sigismond, 15, 60

Thám, Václav, 6

Theatre Association, 44, 45, 47, 48–9

Theodor, Duke Carl, 4

Thörnqvist, Dr Clara, vii, 24n

Thun, Elisabeth von. *See* Kaunitz, Elisabeth

Thun, Count Leopold F., 18, 19

Thun, Countess Maria F., 59

Thun family, 21

Tomášek, Václav Jan Křtitel, 6, 7

Trnobranský, Václav, 136

Trojan, Jan, 2, 3

Tröltsch, Dr, 45

Tůma, František Ignác, 5

Turnovský. *See* Trojan, Jan

Tyl, Josef Kajetán, 7

Ulm, František Baltazar, 30n

Umělecká beseda, 32, 35, 54

Urbánek, František Augustin, 50n, 67n, 76

Valentin, Charlotte, 45

Valentin, J. P., 35

Index

Vaňhal, Jan Křtitel, 5
Velt, Robert, 58
Vejvanovský, Pavel Josef, 3
Venatorini. See Mysliveček
Verdi, Giuseppe, 38
   Un ballo in maschera, 73
Vlček, Vilém, 16
Vojáček, Hynek, 35
   The Captured Maid, 35
Voříšek, Jan Václav (Hugo), 7
Vranický, Antonín, 5
Vranický, Pavel, 5, 8

Wagner, Richard, 39, 96, 98, 116
   Lohengrin, 26
   Das Rheingold, 39
   Tannhäuser, 23, 26
   Tristan and Isolde, 27, 96
   Die Walküre, 39
Wagnerism, 36, 39, 52, 96, 100, 103
Waldstein, Count, 10
Walter, Dr Wenzel, 56n
Wanhal. See Vaňhal
Wassermann, Prof. August von, 151

Weber, Carl Maria von, 5, 15, 28
   Concertstück in F minor, 28
   Der Freischütz, 7, 14, 34, 109
Wehl, A., 94
Weigl, Joseph, 7
Wenzig, Josef, 35, 37, 98, 136, 146
Wieland, Christoph Martin, 137
Windischgrätz, Prince von, 21
Woržischek. See Voříšek
Wranitzky, P. See Vranický, P.

'Ye who are God's Warriors!', 2, 78, 83-4, 103

Záboj (musical album), 28
Zelenka, Jan Dismas, 3
Zelený, Dr Václav Vladimír, 52n, 55, 68, 146
Zeyer, Julius, 81n
Zich, Otakar, 81
Žižka, Jan, 101
Zoufal, Prof. E., 42, 43-4, 45, 46
Züngl, Emanuel, 41, 136
Zvonař, Josef Leopold, 32